BY THE EDITORS OF CONSUMER GUIDE®

GREAT Trucks

BEEKMAN HOUSE
New York

CONTENTS

Louis Weber, President
Publications International, Ltd.
3841 West Oakton Street
Skokie, Illinois 60076

Permission is never granted for commercial purposes.

Manufactured in the United States of America
10 9 8 7 6 5 4 3 2 1

Library of Congress Catalog Card Number: 82-62067

ISBN: 0-517-381141

Principal Author: J. F. J. Kuipers

Jacket Design: Frank E. Peiler

This edition published by:
Beekman House
Distributed by Crown Publishers, Inc.
One Park Avenue
New York, New York 10016

INTRODUCTION

Is driving a truck a romantic life? Most of the time, probably not for the teamsters behind the wheels who have to drive endless miles through rain, snow, freezing cold, and high winds with few of the creature comforts found in most passenger cars and usually with no companions except other truckers on the road. Even then, companionship might be only a brief encounter through a CB radio or over a cup of coffee at a truck stop.

It's a hard life, with long hours at the wheel, many days away from home, and a responsibility to deliver the goods on time, no matter how treacherous the roads get. But it's obviously also a good life, since few truckers would trade their perch high above the road for a soft swivel chair behind a desk. They are the modern cowboys, "real men" who lead a freewheeling life that most desk clerks only dream of. They criss-cross continents regularly, leave one country and enter another as a routine matter, drive from densely populated urban areas to remote rural locales, leaving a hot sun behind them one day and entering arctic cold the next—a life that offers continuous adventure.

Truckers, however, have little time to enjoy the scenery since their main concerns are keeping their rig rollin' and reaching their destination. The glamor of a trucker's life is noticed more by bystanders than by the truckers themselves.

The truck was developed because the growth of the industrial age required a means of transporting goods much faster than a horse could and in much greater loads. The first answer to this need was the train, which could carry people and cargo at high speed. Then came

Above: The first Daimler truck, introduced in 1896. *Right:* 1915 Jeffrey Quad 4 x 4, famous World War I army truck. *Below:* 1926 Ford Model T.

steam powered road locomotives at around 1870, and later experimental steam trucks. The first successful model was the Thorneycroft No. 1 steam van of 1896, followed by a Leyland steam van that same year. Gottlieb Daimler, the German who invented the high-speed internal combustion engine, designed the first gasoline-powered truck.

Daimler exported his invention to France, Britain, and the U.S., where the famous piano manufacturer, Steinway, helped Daimler set up a plant. Building trucks rapidly became big business and companies such as Autocar, International, White, Mack, Reo, Foden, Saurer, Fiat, and Renault entered the industry in its early stages. In those early days steam engines were much more popular in Europe than in the U.S.,

where the gas engine was the preferred powerplant. By the 1930s, most European truck makers were changing to diesel engines because of their strength, durability, and economy.

Long-distance trucking reached full development during the '50s and '60s with the introduction of turbocharged diesels (pioneered by Volvo), tractors made of weight-saving alloy metals, and cab-over-engine designs that challenged the popularity of conventional designs. However, it was in the mid-'70s that the romance and adventure of trucking attracted great attention. During the oil shortage that started in 1973, American truckers became folk heroes as they fought escalating prices and the scarcity of fuel while openly defying the new 55-mph national speed limit.

They popularized the CB radio trying to evade police radar, coining new jargon that warned one another of a "bear in the air" or a "smokey in the grass." Drivers also urged each other to "keep the shiny side up" and advised of traffic and road problems through their electronic network that received widespread publicity in the press and in popular songs.

Trucks and trucking are elements of a very dynamic scene that changes continuously, but never loses its excitement or glamor. The roaring diesels, the colorfully painted cabs, the distant destinations far beyond the horizon give trucking a romantic appeal matched by few other fields. This book is dedicated to the "hardware" of this adventurous life, a collection of great trucks from all over the world.

AVTOEXPORT

Trucking in Russia is trucking under the most difficult conditions. The country is vast, and large areas like Siberia are sparsely inhabited. Most people live either in the far west or the coastal regions, and the mainland can be driven for hours without meeting a soul. A large part of the country lies above the Arctic Circle, which means it is extremely cold nine months of the year. During the other three months the weather feels like what most would call a cold spring. The top of

the soil thaws during those three months, turning into a sea of mud.

No wonder then that many trucks built and used in the USSR are off-road trucks, with all-wheel drive and sturdy construction. The heaviest vehicles manufactured in the USSR are the Kamaz, KrAZ, MAZ, Ural, and ZIL. The Kamaz and MAZ are the only highway models; the other models are tough off-roaders. Among them the Ural is a real giant, a high-sitting mud-plower that wades through water up to five feet deep.

Like most off-road trucks, its payload is very limited, only five tons, though it is capable of hauling gross train weights up to 22 tons. Unique features of Russian trucks are a liquid fuel engine preheater and a liquid fuel cab heater. Still, they aren't considered luxuries in areas where the temperature may drop to –40 degrees Fahrenheit.

The Kamaz is the newest of USSR trucks, built in a gigantic plant on the Kama River that has a capacity of 150,000 trucks annually. Older Russian trucks were patterned after U.S. wartime vehicles. The last of these oldies still being built is the KrAZ, a truck in use all over the world. It's rugged, spartan, and it's available in only one color—green!

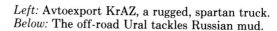

Left: Avtoexport KrAZ, a rugged, spartan truck.
Below: The off-road Ural tackles Russian mud.

4

BEDFORD

You'll probably find Bedford trucks in any country you visit. Based in England, the company is a real cosmopolitan among the world's truck manufacturers. Light and medium trucks are the mainstay of Bedford production, but in recent years they have offered heavy models called the TM with Detroit Diesel engines, good sellers in Britain and on the European continent, but also exported elsewhere. They can be spotted in the deserts of Arab countries, in Asia, and in Africa.

When the TM was launched in 1974 in Europe, it introduced touches of American styling with its short BBC cab, unusual for Europe where cabs were generally mounted right before the front axle instead of above it. The lone exception till then was the heavy Volvo cab-over. The specifications were also very American with Eaton and Rockwell axles, Detroit Diesel and Cummins engines, Lipe clutches, and Fuller gearboxes.

The Bedford TM is a real top-of-the-line truck, a well-equipped, comfortable highway-runner with luxurious day-cabs or sleeper-cabs, popular in Great Britain and also used by many fleet owners and owner/operators on the continent. In Germany they are known as the Bedford Blitz, using a well-established Opel truck name as a foot-in-the-door with German haulers. The Bedford TM is not yet really considered a long-distance truck. It's more commonly used as a truck for short heavy runs, possibly because Bedford only built smaller, lighter trucks until 1974.

The TM series was recently completely re-engineered and overhauled, to make it more suitable for the '80s.

Bedford TJ conventional trucks are very popular in developing countries. In production since 1958, the TJ celebrates its 25th anniversary in 1983. In fact they are medium-weight trucks, but transporters in developing countries can't afford expensive job-rated trucks, so the tiny TJs are used for all sorts of duties, such as hauling a load of lumber for which an American contractor would at least select the smallest conventional Mack, Kenworth, or Peterbilt.

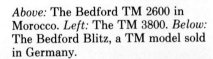

Above: The Bedford TM 2600 in Morocco. *Left:* The TM 3800. *Below:* The Bedford Blitz, a TM model sold in Germany.

DAF

A major power in European trucking is DAF of Holland, manufacturing some 11,000 medium and heavy trucks annually and exporting them to all parts of the world. DAF, one of the youngest major manufacturers, started building trucks in 1950, a year in which most of its competitors had already celebrated their 50th anniversary or were about to. The reason for their quick success is simple: DAF had to fight for a share of a market that already had been divided among a number of large manufacturers. This forced them to be creative, adventurous truck builders whose vehicles were well engineered with low chassis weight, low running costs, and enormous versatility.

The modern DAFs are highly efficient machines, perfectly suited for long-distance trucking under the most arduous conditions. Nearly all components are manufactured by DAF. Only the gearboxes are bought from outside suppliers, among them Fuller. The diesel engines are refined performers, with low fuel consumption through turbocharging and intercoolers, particularly on the more powerful models. The heaviest vehicle currently available is the 3300, a speedy highway runner, but equally suited to tackle extremely heavy short-distance work, such as in the construction business. They are popular with truckers because DAFs are reliable vehicles that keep running and offer a high degree of comfort in large, roomy cabs. They can even be fitted with a small kitchen for those who drive to the Middle East frequently along the so-called Ho-Chi Minh Trail, which has almost as many wrecked trucks on the side of the road as good ones running on it.

International Harvester bought a 32 percent share of DAF in March 1972 and later increased it to 39 percent. The deal was that IH would finance investments, and through DAF would gain a foothold in the European truck market, where they had met with considerable difficulty when they tried it on their own in the '50s. However, the DAF-IH marriage hasn't been a very happy one and it even came to a kind of separation of bed and board when IH also bought a share of Pegaso, a Spanish truck manufacturer and major competitor of DAF.

The latest addition to the DAF line is the conventional Model N 2800, introduced early in 1981, and at first intended for developing countries, where trucks are constantly overloaded and mistreated on poor or nonexistent roads. Survival under such conditions requires a sturdy, spartan truck of extremely strong construction and with a large built-in fuel reserve. Obviously these characteristics are important in other countries, since the N 2800 is currently available in several European markets. The cab-over version is called the MAG 2800. From the jungle of Nigeria to the paved roads of Europe isn't the usual route for introducing a new truck, but if it survived the jungle you know one thing for sure: you're getting a lot of truck for your money.

Above: DAF MAG 2800 C.O.E.
Below: FT 2500 (*left*) and F 3300 (*right*).

DENNISON

For many years the Dennisons of Ireland were renowned manufacturers of trailers and semi-trailers, until they sold this business in 1975 to Fruehauf and decided to build trucks and tractors, becoming the first truck manufacturer on the Emerald Isle. By 1977 they had designed a line of custom-built trucks, using the well-known British Motor Panels cab, also mounted on Foden and Scammell trucks and the heavy Dutch FTF vehicles, and other British parts like Gardner and Rolls Royce diesel engines, and American parts like Eaton axles, Lipe clutches, and Fuller transmissions.

Two or three vehicles were completed per week. Some were exported to Great Britain, but most of them remained in Ireland where the truckers were happy with the quality and performance of the newcomer. In 1979 Dennison mounted a new cab, the Finnish Sisu forward-control unit, a roomy and comfortable driver's perch with lots of glass and plenty of comfort.

However, economic times were getting tougher and exports to Britain failed to meet expectations, so Dennison ran into money trouble. The beauties from the Emerald Isle, with their Scandinavian-style cab, could no longer compete with the more established makes and they ran out of orders. The Dennison truck dreams ended in 1981 and the family-owned business turned its attention again to manufacturing trailers and semi-trailers.

Left: Dennison 8 x 4 with a GCW of 44 tons. *Above:* Early custom-built Dennison with Motor Panels cab.

DIAMOND REO

Diamond Reo Giant conventionals started rolling off the assembly line of Osterlund, Inc., in Harrisburg, Pennsylvania, late in 1977, but the heritage of these trucks goes back nearly 75 years earlier to the formation of the Reo Motor Car Company. The name Reo comes from the company's founder, Ransom E. Olds, of Oldsmobile fame. A few years after Reo started producing trucks, the Diamond T company did also. The two companies combined production in 1959 as the Diamond Reo Division under the ownership of White Motor Company. White sold the company in the early '70s and by 1975 Diamond Reo production had ceased. But two years later, Osterlund had acquired all the manufacturing and marketing rights to the well-known truck name and production of the new Giant series began.

Diamond Reo bills itself as "The World's Toughest Truck" and offers the Giant in three tandem-axle models and one single rear axle model. The trucks can be tailored to serve as rock or aggregate haulers, construction or ready mix trucks, long-haul highway vehicles, and other uses. Standard engines are Cummins 855-cubic-inch diesels with either 240 or 300 HP. Cummins diesels with up to 400 HP are optional. The 6x4 tandem axle models have capacities of up to 29 tons.

Diamond Reo Giant C11664DB conventional, tandem axle model with air-operated steel radiator shutters. Osterlund, Inc. began building Diamond Reos in 1977.

Above: Diamond Reo Giant with "low boy" for heavy construction work. *Left:* Giant C11664DBT. *Below:* Giant cab features a curved panoramic dashboard.

DODGE

Barreiros C 37 C.O.E.

The Spanish Dodge story begins in 1952, when a man called Eduardo Barreiros started producing diesel engines in Madrid. Five years later he was building trucks around these engines, using French Heuliez cabs, the same ones that were also mounted by Berliet of France. However, Barreiros couldn't make it on its own, so AEC of Britain bought a share of the company. But the new alliance lasted only a few years because AEC became part of British Leyland, which cooperated with Spanish Pegaso, and the connections with Barreiros ended. Chrysler of Europe, which already had a manufacturing agreement with Barreiros that allowed him to build Simca and Dodge cars under license, took over a majority of the Barreiros stock and developed a new line of trucks. In Spain they were still offered under the Barreiros name, but for export they were renamed Dodge.

When Chrysler ran into trouble during the late '70s, the company sold its European operations to Peugeot, which for the first time became a manufacturer of heavy trucks (under the Dodge name). The truck business, however, is quite different from the car business, and Peugeot wasn't very successful in this venture. Therefore, negotiations were started to find a partner for the Spanish Dodge truck plant, and also for the British Dodge truck operations. The result was that the French Renault company bought 50 percent of the Spanish and British Dodge truck operations and agreed to manage them. In fact, Renault now controls Dodge in Europe; Peugeot only shares the revenues.

The main advantage of the Dodge trucks is their price, rather low compared with other trucks in this class. Technically, they are of mediocre quality, however, and are fitted with a cab that was outdated when it was introduced; a bulbous, baroque design with lots of frills. Though the Spanish Dodge trucks are sold in other European countries, 95 percent of them are running in Spain.

Left: Dodge 300 Series R3620P with turbo diesel Chrysler engine. *Upper left:* Dodge 300 in service in Holland. *Above:* A 300 Series C 38 with 275 HP in-line 6-cylinder diesel engine.

ERF

During Easter of 1933, when England was in an economic depression, four men made plans in a borrowed greenhouse in Sandbach, Cheshire, to produce a new truck. Among them were two members of the Foden family, famous manufacturers of steam trucks. They had retired from the family company because the change from steam-powered to diesel-powered trucks made it clear that diesel trucks had a future, while steamers had already had their day.

To prove they were right, they designed a truck of their own, using components like Gardner engines, Kirkstal axles, and David Brown gearboxes, which proved quite successful. From these humble beginnings they grew into their current role of Britain's most important independent truck maker. ERF produces B- and C-series trucks, available as two-, three-, and four-axle rigids or two- and three-axle tractors. One feature of the ERFs is their low chassis weight, allowing a relatively high payload. Other features are the very stiff cab, with a steel skeleton paneled with thermo-shaped SMC-panels; the hydraulic tilting pump for the cab that also works as a shock absorber when the cab is returned to its normal position, and a security device that prevents the truck from being driven with insufficient brake air pressure.

The export market is an important one for ERF. Their trucks are used in New Zealand, Australia, the Middle East, Africa, and Asia, where special versions for these export markets are engineered for local conditions. ERF has a manufacturing subsidiary in South Africa, their most important export market. A modified version of the B-series truck is built in South Africa using a locally built variant of a six-cylinder Mercedes diesel engine as the power plant, among others.

All ERFs are more or less custom-built trucks. You can build the vehicle you need by selecting from a detailed list of specifications, though it's not as detailed as what U.S. truck manufacturers offer. But for Britain it is obviously detailed enough. ERF holds a solid 16 percent of the British heavy truck market, enough to make the company prosperous.

Left: ERF built in South Africa.
Above: ERF B-series with 30-ton GVW.

FAP

Fabrika Automobila Priboj was founded 30 years ago in Yugoslavia, which at that time was still recovering from World War II. Driving over Yugoslav roads in those days was a matter of jolting from one hole to another. The country's roads were paved with cobblestones, a roadbuilding material that truckers hate because it can rattle a truck into pieces and jar the driver's kidneys. With many cobblestones missing, the postwar Yugoslav roads really were a mess, and it was FAP's task to design a truck that could cope with those conditions. FAP needed a partner and chose Saurer of Austria, a company that had earned a reputation for building trucks that could stand up to severe operating conditions. The Austrian Saurer company, associated with the Swiss Saurer company, helped FAP design a line of cab-over and conventional trucks fitted with sturdy diesel engines. They were trucks that had little trouble with the difficult Yugoslav roads and they proved to be matchless in safety, reliability, and endurance.

FAPs are still manufactured at Priboj, but the design has changed to meet modern requirements. Most of these trucks do service in Yugoslavia.

However, it looks as if the days of the original FAPs are numbered. A few years ago the company reached agreement with Daimler-Benz that allows FAP to use the Daimler-Benz cab and licenses production of modern Mercedes engines by the FAMOS engine manufacturing subsidiary of FAP. Three FAPs based on Mercedes patents are currently in production (the 1616, the 1620, and the 2026) and it is to be expected that more will follow, marking the end of an era.

FAP 15, powered by 160 HP diesel.

FAP 18 has 38-ton GCW.

FAUN

The Faun works of Lauf an der Pegnitz are the oldest German manufacturers of trucks. Since about 1900 Faun has built special vehicles such as municipal and fire-fighting trucks, along with regular trucks. Faun street sweepers, sanitation trucks, and vacuum trucks were used in many European cities before 1940.

The special vehicle business became so important that Faun decided to concentrate on that area during the late '60s. The only leftover from the truck days is a line of heavy truck tractors for moving bulky loads, use on oil fields, as military tank transporters, and off-road hauling. Faun offers a choice of normal and forward control models, with two, three, four, or five axles. Every truck tractor is custom built, using engines from Cummins, Detroit Diesel, MAN, Mercedes, Deutz, or MTU. Since gearshifting is hard work, the heaviest models that tow up to 60 tons can be fitted with an Allison automatic gearbox and torque converter.

Fauns are used all over the world. Trucks are also derived from the truck tractors, particularly for oil field use, with long self-loading platform bodies and winches. Most are fitted with all-wheel drive, which usually means five driven axles. These axles are built by Faun, and provide high dynamic carrying capacity. They are built to take high-torque input and offer high final reduction ratios by planetary gear sets in the wheel hubs. In most cases the dead weight of a heavy prime mover will be doubled or even tripled by adding ballast to get enough rolling friction, which means that the axles must have a carrying capacity far exceeding the weight of the tractor. About 1000 Faun truck tractors are sold each year.

Faun HZ 36.40/45 6 x 6 *(left)* and HZ 32.25/40 6 x 6 *(right)* can move huge, bulky loads.

FBW

Franz Brozicevic of Wetzikon, Switzerland, started building trucks under the Franz name in 1911, launching the first European five-tonner with shaft drive. It was a sturdy vehicle, well constructed and extremely long lasting. These characteristics were typical of every FBW, as they were later named, and it was the reason that Henschel of Kassel, Germany, later contracted to build FBW trucks under license in Germany.

FBW has never produced series; instead they make individually tailored trucks, but use only components they manufacture themselves. Engines, gearboxes, and axles are all of their own design and production, a costly system given the fact that FBW produces only a few hundred vehicles per year. But their quality is such that their trucks might last twice as long as an average truck. An unwanted consequence is that the market for FBW trucks is limited. They have a small circle of loyal clients who are willing to pay more for an excellent truck, but after selling one, the FBW people have to wait twice as long before they see the customer again.

It wasn't surprising then that they ran into financial trouble a few years ago. The FBW company was taken over by Oerlikon Buhrle, a large Swiss engineering group, which tried to increase production but with little result. As a next step contacts were sought with Daimler-Benz of Germany to enhance their prospects of taking over FBW. A deal was struck giving Mercedes a 50 percent share of FBW, which would start producing eight-wheelers for Mercedes, at first in addition to their own lines. From 1983 on FBW will produce only Mercedes-designed trucks and their own truck production will be discontinued by that date.

To many, that is a pity. It will mean that the famous FBW underfloor truck, manufactured since 1949, will be a thing of the past. It also means the end of the line for the FBW conventional trucks, sturdy vehicles, in most cases with all-wheel drive. They could climb the Alps like mountain goats while pulling loads of 100 tons or more.

FBW F 923 8 x 4; GCW 80 tons.

FBW U 519 with under-floor engine.

FODEN

Foden's cab-over-engine models have included the S 104 *(right)*; the newer S 106, painted American style *(lower right)*; and the S 83 *(below)*. Foden now concentrates on custom building.

Just a few miles down the same road at Sandbach where ERF trucks are built is another British independent truck manufacturer, Foden. That is not just a coincidence. Foden, a family company, was established in Sandbach in 1887. However, during the early '30s the family split up. Two of the Fodens, Edwin and his son Dennis, founded ERF. The rest of the family eventually changed the Foden business from building steam vehicles into a manufacturer of diesel-powered vehicles.

The first Foden diesel truck was powered by a Gardner diesel engine, the start of an agreement that still

exists, though Foden for some time during the '50s and '60s also offered its own two-stroke diesel engine, which could be easily identified by its screaming sound.

Foden ran into financial trouble in 1980 and was subsequently bought by the American Paccar group, which reshaped the company into a real custom builder. Production changed to a smaller scale than Foden had been used to.

When Foden introduced its Universal and Fleetmaster lines in 1977 for export markets, it adopted a simplified spare parts system that relied on major component suppliers such as Lipe, Rockwell, Fuller,

Rolls-Royce, and Cummins. That meant parts were more readily available for trucks used outside Britain. The same system is used in the current Foden models, the Fleetmaster and Haulmaster, which use a wide range of Cummins, Rolls-Royce, and Gardner diesel engines, Fuller transmissions, and Rockwell axles. The cabs are, in the best Foden tradition, still made of fiberglass. Production is concentrated on heavy models of at least 32 tons gross train weight, two- and three-axle tractors, and three- and four-axle trucks. Those who want a fancy paint job in the American style shouldn't hesitate to ask.

FORD

Ford has been into trucking since 1911, when commercial roadsters and delivery vans based on the venerable Model T passenger car were first offered for sale. From these lightweight vehicles, whose modest payloads were frequently surpassed, Ford's offerings grew with the trucking industry and by 1936 the company had produced 3 million trucks. Whether it was a small delivery vehicle, or a giant highway model, Ford was building them through the '40s, '50s, and '60s. Ford's truck program took a significant turn in 1970 when the Louisville line was launched. It was an entirely new range of medium- and heavy-duty trucks filling the gap between the F-series and the W-range, and one of the broadest Ford had ever offered with single- and tandem-axle trucks and tractors, long and short hoods on conventional models, and versions with a setback front axle. A new plant was built (in Louisville, Kentucky, of course) to produce these trucks and at that time it was the largest truck plant in the world. It remains one of the largest.

After 12 years of production the Louisville line, or L-line as they are better known, is still a bestseller, offering a choice of more than 650 models, not including the latest LTL. Louisvilles have been accepted as durable and reliable heavy trucks, with excellent performance and economical operation.

An assembly operation for Louisvilles opened in Australia in 1975 at the Ford Broadmeadows truck plant. The Louisvilles were revised and adapted to Australian conditions, which are very different from those in America. For the trucker, the Louisvilles offer premium comfort both in the U.S. and the Australian versions with Cush-N-Aire driver's seat, excellent instrumentation, an adjustable steering column, and substantial ergonomic engineering.

The Louisville also influenced Ford truck manufacturing in Europe. Until the mid-'70s the Ford subsidiaries in England and Germany produced only light- and medium-duty trucks (for example, the Thames Trader and D-range), but in 1975 Ford of Europe entered the heavy-duty market with the Transcontinental line, a custom-built truck offering several choices in power plants, transmissions, and axles. Backbone of the Transcontinental is the chassis frame used on the Louisville line, made from high-grade steel. The cab used is purchased from Renault in France and is the same one used on Renault's heavy models. Transcontinentals initially were assembled at the Amsterdam Ford plant, but during 1981 production was transferred to the British Foden plant at Sandbach.

Though the Transcontinental is an interesting truck, with fine performance, superb ride and handling, and many other positive points, Ford never reached its goal of selling 7000 trucks a year in Europe by 1980. As a newcomer they were unable to snatch away substantial market shares from the well-established heavy truck manufacturers. In fact, Ford couldn't match its direct competitor, the Bedford TM. The American line of Ford trucks has expanded with two new models, the CL-9000 cab-over and the LTL-9000 conventional, which had special appeal for the owner-operator. The CL-9000 is a sophisticated truck, with advanced engineering under the skin and lots of comfort for the long-distance driver who had to spend many consecutive days and nights in his truck. For those perferring a conventional truck the LTL-9000 offers the same comfort and engineering.

Ford also manufactures trucks in Brazil where a whole range of vehicles based on the American F-types are produced. Among them are a number of heavies, such as the F 7 and F 8. They are available with gas engines, or with Detroit Diesel engines up to about 200 HP.

The Transcontinental 4432, part of Ford's heavy truck line that has been marketed in Europe.

Above: An LTL-9000, newest conventional in Ford's Louisville series, rolls off the Kentucky assembly line. *Right:* the CL-9000, Ford's latest heavy C.O.E. *Below:* Brazilian F 8500 in logging service.

Top: Ford Transcontinental 4435, part of the European line. *Above left:* Australian version of a Louisville conventional. *Above right:* American LT conventional. *Right:* The majestic and regal LTL-9000, with fully equipped sleeper compartment.

FREIGHTLINER

onsolidated Freightways of Salt Lake City, Utah, decided in 1939 it needed a new breed of trucks to remain a competitive shipping firm. They wanted lighter vehicles that would haul a bigger payload per run. Since these trucks weren't available, they designed one themselves—the prototype of the Freightliner. Production didn't start until 1947 because World War II forced a delay in their plans, but in that year five men started building a lightweight cab-over truck at a small Portland, Oregon, plant, delivering a few trucks each month to Consolidated Freightways.

The quality of these first Freightliners was such that many other truckers quickly became interested in them, which led to a decision to market the Freightliners commercially. A sales agreement with White Motor Co. allowed them to sell Freightliner trucks as White-Freightliners through their sales outlets, and at the same time obligating White to take care of the after-sales service. This agreement lasted to 1977, when Freightliner continued on page 33

Above: Freightliner conventional, smart-looking and built for the open road.

Below: Freightliner cab-over, known for its alloy construction.

Left: Avtoexport Kamaz (U.S.S.R.) *Below:* Bedford TM4400 (England)

Above: Chevrolet Medium-Duty Conventional (U.S.A.) *Near right:* Chevrolet Kodiak Medium-Duty Conventional (U.S.A.) *Far right:* DAF 2800 C.O.E. (Netherlands) *Below:* DAF Model N (Netherlands)

Near right: Dennison C.O.E. (Ireland) *Below:* Dodge C-17 C.O.E. (Netherlands) *Far right:* ERF C 32-4 C.O.E. (England) *Lower right:* ERF 66Cu C.O.E. (South Africa)

Page opposite: Above left: FAP 1619 BDT C.O.E. (Yugoslavia) *Above right:* Faun HZ 5060 Conventional (Germany) *Center:* Foden S 106 C.O.E. (England) *This page: Top:* Ford LTL-9000 Conventional (U.S.A.) *Left:* Ford L-700 Medium-Duty Conventional (U.S.A.) *Above:* Ford F-Series Medium-Duty Conventional (U.S.A.)

Page opposite: *Above:* Ford CL-9000 C.O.E. (U.S.A.)
Below: Ford Transcontinental C.O.E. (England) *This page:*
Left: Freightliner C.O.E. (U.S.A.) *Below:* FWD Trac-
tioneer Conventional (U.S.A.) *Bottom:* F.T.F. Turbo
(Netherlands)

This page: *Above:* GMC Astro 95 C.O.E. (U.S.A.) *Right:* GMC Brigadier Heavy-Duty Conventional (U.S.A.) *Below:* Hino HE C.O.E. (Japan) *Page opposite: Top:* International Eagle Brougham Conventional (U.S.A.) *Middle left:* International Paystar Conventional (U.S.A.) *Middle right:* International Eagle C.O.E. (U.S.A.) *Lower left:* International Paystar 5000 Conventional. *Lower right:* International ACCO 1880 (Australia)

Left: Fiat 190 C.O.E. (Italy) *Upper left:* Isuzu VSR C.O.E. (Japan) *Upper right:* Kaelble KDVW 421 ZW C.O.E. (Germany) *Above:* Jelcz 316 C.O.E. (Poland) *Below:* IVECO-Magirus 190 Turbo C.O.E. (Germany)

Page opposite: Upper left: Kenworth Transorient C.O.E. (Australia) *Upper right:* Kenworth W900 SAR Conventional (Australia) *Bottom:* Leader C.O.E. (Australia) *This page: Left:* Leyland Roadtrain C.O.E. (England) *Below:* Liaz-Skoda S100 05 C.O.E. (Czechoslovakia) *Bottom left:* Mack's new Ultra-Liner C.O.E. for 1983 (U.S.A.) *Bottom right:* Mack Mid-Liner MS 200 C.O.E. (France/U.S.A.)

Above: Mack Super-Liner Conventional (U.S.A.) *Right:* Mack Model R Conventional (U.S.A.)

Above: Freightliner's contemporary models in conventional and C.O.E. styles. *Below:* A cab-over from the days when Freightliner was partners with White.

continued from page 16
organized its own sales and service system, and at the same time supplemented its own trucks with a number of light- and medium-weight models from Volvo.

Freightliner currently manufactures cab-over-engine and conventional trucks. Both are custom made and offer a greater payload than any other truck in Class B through the use of aluminum alloy in the construction. This is why Freightliners aren't among the cheapest trucks on the market, but

they can earn more dollars per trip despite this price disadvantage because of greater payload. About 8,000 Freightliners are sold annually, most of them to owner/operators, who appreciate the Freightliner's construction advantages and its luxurious interior that offers premium-grade comfort over long distances.

The basic lines of the Freightliner cab-over date from the early '50s; they have been only slightly reshaped since then. The conventional model hasn't had any cosmetic alteration

since its introduction in 1974. In this respect Freightliner clearly is the exception to the American rule that every new model year should bring at least subtle changes.

The ties between Volvo and Freightliner have recently been cut and Freightliner is now owned by Mercedes, though few truckers will notice that in everyday contact with the company. Freightliner will keep its own identity. The main change is that Freightliner dealers are no longer selling Volvos as an additional line, and now offer Mercedes instead.

FTF

The FTF is a Dutch truck made since 1966 by Floor of Wychen, a company that had imported the American Mack for about 16 years. After analyzing its situation during the '60s, the company concluded it would be more profitable to build a complete Mack-like truck in Holland than to import Macks into Holland and assemble them there.

Thus it was that the first FTFs had a lot of the Mack technique under the hood. Gradually, however, it was replaced by other components like Detroit Diesel and Cummins engines, Fuller gearboxes, and Rockwell axles.

During the late '60s a second generation of FTF trucks was introduced using cabs by Motor Panels of Coventry, England, and generally American components. These were assembled by pure custom-building: the client could specify his requirements and FTF would build a truck to match them, though from a rather limited

selection of components. Two-, three-, four-, and five-axle trucks and tractors are manufactured by FTF. They can pull up to about 200 tons, and are frequently used on specialized jobs like the transport of heavy, bulky loads, logging, earthmoving, and construction. Many are fitted with Allison automatic gearboxes. FTF often specifies them as standard equipment and offers Fuller multi-speed boxes as an option. The chassis-frames of the FTF trucks are built up in sections

forged from American manganese steel. FTFs are really Dutch trucks; they're rarely seen outside Holland. During 1980 a new range of FTF trucks, their third generation, was introduced. Technically, they are about the same as the second generation, but with a new, up-to-date and luxurious cab also produced by Motor Panels of Coventry. About 100 units are built by hand per year, enough to cope with the special transport demands of the Dutch.

Left: FTF 8.28 cab-over truck. *Below:* FTF 8.8.20 DS tractor.

FWD

Since FWD was started in 1912, its main product has been all-wheel-drive trucks that can go almost anywhere. One of the first to find that out was Gen. John Pershing, who used a fleet of the early FWDs on a crusade into Mexico, through deserts, prairies, and wild streams chasing Pancho Villa's bandit gang. Pershing reported that the FWD trucks were superior to all other trucks used in the Mexican campaign.

Since those days, rugged construction has been a selling point of FWD trucks, even the over-the-road tractors built during the '70s that failed to gain a profitable share of the market. By 1974 FWD decided to concentrate again on all-wheel-drive trucks and crane carriers and stopped building road tractors.

FWD, based in Wisconsin, currently offers the brawny

Tractioneers, efficient off-road vehicles that can cope with the most fearsome conditions. The Tractioneer line is divided into two series, the RB, intended for highway maintenance and jobs like snow removal, and the CB, for civilian uses such as concrete mixers, on oil fields, on construction and mining sites, and other rough jobs. Major parts like axles, transfer boxes, and differential locks are manufactured by FWD to ensure reliability. The engines are

diesels from Detroit Diesel, Allison, or Cummins, ranging in output up to 435 HP.

FWDs are huge, impressive vehicles, basically of 6x6 configuration, but often fitted with additional pusher and tag axles around the rear tandem, thus forming majestic 10x6 units. About 1000 vehicles are built each year.

FWD Tractioneer RB, a specialty truck for highway maintenance.

GMC

Along with Ford and International, GMC dominates the American truck market. Some 75 percent of all trucks sold in the U.S. are manufactured by these three, including GMCs sold under the Chevrolet nameplate. All three entered the heavy-duty field late. GMC's aluminum tilt cab models debuted in the early '60s and have been quite successful, giving GMC a considerable piece of the heavy duty truck market.

GMC's second generation, introduced in 1967 as the Astro, is a cab-over that was quite popular among owner/operators. To get an even larger share of this very important market, GMC launched two new models in 1977: the conventional General and the SS-version of the Astro. Both were loaded with luxuries and conveniences, marking the company's entry into the top league of the truck market. GMC's competitor in the smaller cab-over market is the Brigadier, with a short BBC measurement of 92 inches, against 108 inches for the General. The Brigadier is in fact an upgraded version of the 8000 and 9500 conventionals, using the same running gear, but a more luxurious cab with a brawny hood made of fiberglass. (All these heavy GMCs were also available with the Chevrolet badge up to 1981. However, since then Chevrolet has concentrated on its traditional market, the light and medium trucks.) The heavy-duty models—Brigadier, General and Astro—are impressive trucks, well-engineered and able to perform capably under all circumstances: long-distance runs, bulk hauling, logging, construction, and the refuse industry.

GMC introduced the Dragfoiler aerodynamic air deflector in the mid-'70s, mounted as an option on the cab roofs of the heaviest models to reduce fuel consumption. It cuts wind resistance of a tractor-trailer combination, requiring less power to run the vehicle at highway speed, and improving fuel economy. The device was developed at the GM laboratories and tested in wind tunnels and on the road before it became a production option in the mid-'70s.

GMC Astros are now fitted with fuel-efficient turbocharged diesels. The turbos are frequently used with intercoolers that cool the air after it has passed through the turbochargers for greater efficiency and power.

GMC Brigadier, one of the smaller heavyweights from General Motors.

GMC also takes good care of the driver. The General cab is on a soft-ride mount, using an adjustable air spring and shock absorber at the rear mounting point instead of the usual rubber cushion. A control valve in the cab allows the driver to adjust pressure for maximum riding comfort under all conditions.

Astro, General and Brigadier all are custom-built models. The buyer selects what he wants from a vast range of possibilities. If you are an owner/operator and want something out of the ordinary in the convenience area, select the Five Star treatment for your General, or the Special treatment for your Astro. Brigadier owners can choose from three dress-up packages: one for the exterior that has chrome bumpers, stainless steel West Coast mirrors, and more; another package that gives the chassis a beauty treatment with stainless steel quarter fenders and bright fuel tank straps; and a third package that makes the cab cosier by fitting carpeting, dual armrests, and a more attractive dashboard. Since its introduction in 1967, more than 100,000 GMC Astros have been built (including the identical Chevrolet Titan), and there are no signs that this success won't continue.

The Astro, GMC's popular heavyweight. All 1982 Astros are turbocharged.

Top: Heavy-duty GMC General with Five Star trim. *Above:* Cab-over Astro hauling tank trailer. *Right:* General fitted with extra large bumper incorporating a winch for use as a wrecker.

HENDRICKSON

Outside the Chicago area Hendrickson is mainly known as a manufacturer of tandem suspensions, used by nearly every U.S. heavy truck manufacturer, and many abroad. But around Chicago they are also known for their super-class of custom trucks. Since 1913 Hendrickson has built trucks and tractors and all kinds of specialized vehicles that are sold under their own brand name, or as International trucks. They did a good deal of subcontracting work for International, building tandem-axle units during the '30s, for example.

Hendrickson doesn't mass-produce trucks. The company has a small plant and a handful of well-trained employees who can build any kind of truck needed, be it aircraft refuellers, yard jockeys, vehicles for specialized jobs, or fire engines. They will manufacture whatever an operator needs, in a single unit or as a complete fleet.

The Hendrickson highway vehicles are of the H-4 type, offering a lot of engine, axle, and transmission

options, and featuring a cab and engine hood purchased from International. Hendricksons haul everything, general freight, tankers, cattle, grain, gravel, from every place and under all conditions.

Hendrickson H-3, from the small custom builder outside Chicago that also is widely known for its tandem suspensions.

HINO

Some 60 years ago the predecessors of what eventually would become the Hino Motor Co. started building trucks in Japan and in 1946 the Hino Motor Co. was formed. In 1966 an agreement with Toyota made Hino the heavy truck manufacturing arm of the Toyota group, marking the beginning of a broad expansion scheme. Distributors were organized in several countries, and assembly and manufacturing subsidiaries were established in Holland, Norway, and other countries. After the Japanese car manufacturers successfully invaded the world car market, Hino tried to follow this with trucks, but with only modest success.

Hino's light truck models gained some territory in major markets abroad, but its heavy trucks could only penetrate markets in Third World countries and in a few European countries like Ireland and Norway. Hino trucks, like most Japanese trucks, are well-made vehicles that feature modern

innovation under the hood, but nevertheless they were unable to become an important force in most foreign markets.

Hino manufactures a broad range of normal and forward-control trucks, fitted with a variety of engines and axles that enable them to offer vehicles for many purposes. Custom building isn't done in Japan. All

The Hino HE *(right)* and the Hino ZM *(below),* two cab-over-engine models from Toyota's heavy-truck group.

vehicles are manufactured on an assembly line, the number of variations is restricted, and each variation is indicated by letter identification. Trucking in Japan is largely an owner/operator business and hardly any transport companies exist. Owner/operators do the job cheaper, and they do it quickly; 70 mph is a common cruising speed.

INTERNATIONAL

If there is one truck manufacturer whose name perfectly describes its realm, it is International. The company really is international, manufacturing trucks in the U.S., Canada, Australia, and under license in Mexico and Turkey. Furthermore, International Harvester owns Seddon Atkinson, the famous British truck builder, holds a 39 percent stake in DAF of Holland, and maintains assembly plants in other countries.

Despite all this, IH is presently in a precarious financial position. The recession has hurt their sales greatly. The International people are trying to regain their top position in the industry by introducing new generations of trucks, modern manufacturing techniques, and advising fleet owners and owner/operators on maintenance with sophisticated computer technology.

Currently manufactured by the U.S. International Truck Group are the S-line, introduced in 1977 to replace the Loadstar series, and the XL cab-overs, Transtar conventionals, the Paystar construction trucks, and the Cargostar medium-duty models for urban applications.

Of all the new truck lines introduced during the late '70s by U.S. manufacturers, the S-line is by far the most successful. From the first moment it has been a top seller, which is not surprising since the S-line comes in 60 basic models, which can be adapted to any job by selecting the right components from a long list of options. In fact, the S-line ("S" is for the Springfield, Ohio, plant where most of these trucks are built) is the first custom-built unit among the medium and lower gross vehicle weight of the heavyweight

Plush and flashy, International's top-shelf Transtar is the Eagle Brougham.

class. The S-line features innovative engineering under the hood and the design of the vehicle is clean, timeless, and appealing.

The latest additions to the line are the XL cab-overs, introduced in 1980 to compete with the Ford CL and GMC Astro. One strong point of the XL is a claimed improvement in fuel economy of about 10 percent over the Transtar it replaced with an aerodynamic cab design, the use of an IH air deflector as an option, reduced weight, and more efficient powertrain components. Primarily intended for owner/operators is the very luxurious Eagle version of the XL, fitted with a plush interior, many gadgets, and flashy exterior paint schemes.

The conventional companion of the XL is the Transtar, introduced in 1973, and also available in an Eagle version since about 1978. In the Eagle it offers extensive luxury and a roomy cab. Power for the XL and Transtar comes from Detroit Diesel, Caterpillar, and Cummins diesel engines, from 290 to 525 HP output. Gearboxes with up to 20 speeds can be selected from the Fuller and Spicer offerings.

Heavy-duty Internationals are built at IH's heavy vehicle plant at Waggoner, Oklahoma, also the home of that giant truck launched in 1972, the International Paystar. These premium-duty conventionals are for construction, oil field exploration, and mining and are available in 4x4, 6x4, and 6x6 configurations. An 8x4 with front tandem has been developed for oil field rigging operations. A special low-weight version of the Paystar with fiberglass hood has been constructed for California haulers. The intermediate heavyweights of International are the top models in the S-series, the S 2500 and the S 2600, available with IH's own midrange diesel engines, or with powerplants from Detroit Diesel and Cummins.

The S 2600 also is built in Australia by an IH subsidiary, though

the Australian model is different from the original. When the first prototypes arrived in Australia, they were disassembled, and the components tortured under the most severe conditions at the Anglesea Proving Ground of IH. A batch of pre-production models was then loaned to Australian truck operators, who tried them on the roads, which are tougher in Australia than in the U.S. When all this testing was successfully completed, the S-line was introduced to the market in 1980. Besides the S 2600, the normal control Transtar is also manufactured in Australia, using U.S. made cab shells similar to those on the S 2600, but most of the other components are Australian-made by subsidiaries of well-known U.S. component manufacturers.

International trucks can also be found in Mexico, where they are built under license by DINA and FAMSA; and in Turkey, where the Loadstar is still built for local heavy work. The Australian forward control models are also available in New Zealand and in South Africa, where they are assembled (as is the S-line) from American parts. All these trucks are constructed with one thought in mind: life can be tough, so International trucks also have to be tough.

Opposite page: CO-9670 XL *(top),* the impressive Transtar 4300 *(lower left),* and the S-2200 *(lower right). This page:* Australian S-series model *(top left),* midrange S-2600 *(top right),* Aussie 1600 model *(right),* and the super-duty Paystar 5000 *(below).*

ISUZU

The history of Isuzu goes back to 1916, when the Japanese shipbuilding firm of Tokyo Ishikawajima started manufacturing cars and commercial vehicles under license from the British Wolseley company. Long after Wolseley stopped building trucks in England, they were still manufactured under that name in Japan.

The Isuzu name was adopted in 1939 and the company developed into a major manufacturer of trucks and diesel engines after World War II, exporting to many countries in Asia. By the end of the '60s, the major U.S. manufacturers were forging footholds in Japan by buying minority interests in Japanese companies. Thus, Isuzu became a partner of General Motors. The

results of these international marriages were different than envisioned by the U.S. manufacturers who hoped to gain a preferential position in Japan. Instead, the Japanese got the chance to market some of their vehicles worldwide through the distribution networks of the U.S. giants. Thus, Isuzu trucks were offered on the Australian market through Holden and on other local markets through GM sales subsidiaries, at first usually under the Bedford-Isuzu name, but now as Isuzu.

Isuzu trucks marketed worldwide include the conventional T-ranges, heavy-duty workhorses in 4x2, 6x2, or 6x4 configuration. They have won enviable reputations, particularly in Third World countries, for their performance and reliability. They are powered by six-cylinder engines of 204 or 230 HP, able to move at high speed with GVWs up to 24 tons. The all-wheel-drive versions of the

T-range, the T3D 4x4 and the TWD 6x6, have a special military-look engine hood. An unusual feature of these vehicles is the split-type front driving axle, like those used on wartime GMC trucks.

The heaviest types made by Isuzu are the S and V ranges, both cab-overs powered by diesel engines of 204, 230 or 292 HP, and able to move gross train weights up to 45 tons. The cab is an attractive modern structure, roomy, comfortable, and with a well-designed dashboard. Japanese vehicles, including trucks, are known for their technical innovations. Isuzu trucks powered by a V-10 engine are equipped with an anti-white smoke button, for example, that cuts the fuel supply to one of the cylinder banks, making clean, quiet warmups possible without foul odors. Another technical feature is an engine cranking device that can be used when the cab is tilted.

Left: The workhorse Isuzu TDJ.
Above: The heavier SSZ features a roomy cab. *Below:* The heavy-duty VSR C.O.E.

IVECO

Fiat's long history includes ties with several other major European truck manufacturers. Fiat acquired the Italian OM company, a manufacturer of trucks and buses, in 1939 but allowed it to operate independently up to the late '60s. Meanwhile, Fiat also acquired Lancia, which owned a truck factory at Bolzano, and took over the French Unic company from Simca. All these makes at that time had their own lines of vehicles, using their own engines, gearboxes, and axles, and marketed through their own sales networks. This created much duplication in a conglomerate that obviously needed streamlining, so a new company called Fiat Veicoli Industriali was created incorporating Fiat, Lancia and OM, and Unic SA. They all sold the same line of vehicles from light duty to heavy duty, but manufacturing was divided among them, each plant concentrating on certain types of vehicles.

In 1975 the truck manufacturing

activities of the German Klockner-Humboldt-Deutz group (parent company of Magirus-Deutz) were merged with the Fiat group to form a new company, IVECO BV, short for Industrial Vehicles Corporation. Thus Magirus was the last of the five makes to join the combine. Initially, Klockner-Humboldt-Deutz held 29 percent of IVECO, but they sold it in 1981 to Fiat, which became the sole proprietor of IVECO, adding truck manufacturing activities in Brazil and Argentina to the giant company.

The acquisition of Magirus bolstered the IVECO line with the famous German-made conventionals, rugged and sturdy off-roaders for construction and other tough applications. Previously they were available only with air-cooled Deutz engines. Now, however the main models, 4x2, 4x4, 6x4, and 6x6 are also available with a Fiat water-cooled diesel and were added to the OM, Fiat and Unic lines of trucks. Production of the conventionals is concentrated at the Magirus plant in Ulm, West Germany, where the medium-weight Magiruses are also produced, including the special export model

OM 190 Turbo bearing the parent company nameplate, IVECO.

for the U.S. with a Fiat diesel engine. Magirus cab-over production was discontinued. Instead, heavy models of Fiat, OM, and Unic with forward control cab were built with an air-cooled Deutz diesel engine and sold under the Magirus nameplate. Thus five great truck names ended up as five examples of badge engineering.

The IVECO nameplate at first was an inconspicuous addition to the grilles of its trucks, while the original marque badges were still displayed more prominently. The IVECO name now dominates the grilles and the Fiat, OM, Unic, and Magirus badges have been made smaller. The reason for this is that all sales operations have been shifted to IVECO subsidiaries and there are no longer distributors for the separate makes. For example, IVECO Great Britain handles both the Fiat and Magirus lines and IVECO France sells Unic and Magirus.

Though IVECO is the second largest truck manufacturer in

Europe, their trucks are technically rather mediocre, except for the Magirus-made vehicles, which are still superb. Strong points of the Magiruses are their air-cooled engines that perform admirably under all climatic conditions, and the robust construction, a must for construction and other off-road jobs. Magirus air-cooled engines range up to 400 HP and most of them are normally aspirated.

The IVECO 170 and 190 lines, the heaviest vehicles from the group, are powered by a 268 HP turbocharged V-8 air-cooled diesel. These models are produced at the Fiat SpA plant at Turin. Except for the engine, they are identical no matter which nameplate is carried on the front. Only the Magirus version uses the air-cooled diesel engine.

Magirus-made IVECO with Deutz engine *(below)* and a Fiat 170 *(bottom)*.

JELCZ

Polish-built Jelcz S 420 *(left)* and the Jelcz W 640 *(above)*.

Jelczanskie Zaklady Samochodowe, as the company is formally named, is Poland's only manufacturer of heavy trucks, both for over-the-road and off-road uses. Like most Eastern European truck manufacturers, they work under licenses from Western companies. Jelcz mounts engines that are built under Leyland license. Jelcz trucks are very spartan, offering no luxury features and are built to do a tough job and haul goods under the worst climatic conditions and over the worst roads.

Jelcz currently manufactures two lines of trucks, the S 420/S 620 line and the 316/317 line that began in 1952, the year Jelcz started building trucks. Construction and design of the 316/317 have been brought up to modern standards. Since Polish trucks are frequently operated by four-person crews, the Jelcz 316/317 models are equipped with cabs that can seat four. For long-distance trucking, a sleeping berth can be installed as well. The inline six-cylinder diesel engine produces 200 HP, but a more powerful 240 HP engine is available as an option. Gross combination weight of the

vehicle is 32 tons and it can carry 8 tons.

Of more recent construction is the S 420, and the tandem axle companion model S 620. Both are powered by the 240 HP diesel engine, mounted in front of the setback front axle. Features of the S 420 are a longer loading space, a higher cab with improved visibility, and a high ground clearance that makes the vehicle suitable for rough territories. The S 620 version has a payload of 10 tons. The vehicle, used mainly as a tipper for construction work, is fitted with a three-way tipping body.

KAELBLE

Kaelble of Germany built its first heavy vehicle in 1906, a steam-powered road locomotive that started a long history of truck and tractor manufacturing that includes the world's first diesel-engined truck-tractor in 1925, and a giant forward-control prime mover in 1938. The mid-engine jumbo had six drive wheels and two steerable axles, the front axle and the last axle from the tandem, and a 180 HP diesel engine that could pull 22 tons. Today's jumbos from Kaelble are powered by

engines up to 800 HP and are able to haul loads up to some 400 tons with a single tractor.

Kaelble has a strong market in Eastern European countries (the Moscow fire department uses Kaelble ladder trucks) and in the Middle East.

In total, Kaelble builds 16 different models of truck-tractors, with two, three or four axles, all of them all-wheel-drive models. They mount diesel engines from Mercedes-Benz, MAN or MTU (short for Motoren & Turbinen Union, the former Maybach engine works, now jointly owned by Mercedes and MAN), and gearboxes from ZF and Allison. Deutz air-cooled diesel engines are optional

in a number of models, while Voith Power Shift transmissions can replace the Allison automatic gearbox. The axles, built by Kaelble, are heavy-duty pieces of the same kind used in their earth movers and dumptrucks. Though some Kaelble tractors weigh as much as 27 tons, they can exceed 45 mph unloaded. A major user of Kaelble truck-tractors is the German Railway Corporation, which has a road transport division for hauling heavy, extremely large loads. They have used Kaelble vehicles exclusively during the past 50 years for those heavy jobs.

Kaelble KDVW 400 S *(left)* and the KDVW 421 Z *(right)*.

KENWORTH

This page: Mexican-built Kenworth *(above)* and a K 100 C.O.E. in service in Europe. *Opposite page:* New for '82, the W 900 is Kenworth's top-line conventional model, well suited for long-distance hauling.

The beginnings of Kenworth go back to the days when the logging trade of the Pacific Northwest relied on horsepower delivered through hooves instead of tires. Roads as we know them today didn't exist. Old dirt trails were the tracks along which the loads of timber had to be moved along to civilization. The challenge of engineering a truck that could cope with this situation was taken up by the Gerlinger company, the truck manufacturer from which Kenworth descended in 1923. The Gerlinger operation wasn't very successful, but after it was renamed Kenworth and a serious effort was made to build quality trucks, changes came quickly. The company moved to Seattle and Kenworth grew into a custom builder. In 1944 the company became a subsidiary of the Pacific Car & Foundry Company, the start of a new era of expansion leading to the situation today. Kenworth builds trucks in four countries—the U.S., Canada, Mexico, and Australia. Their trucks are of such quality that they have become a standard against which other heavy-duty trucks are measured.

Kenworth is still a prime supplier of heavy trucks for timber hauling, the oil industry, mining, and quarrying. The company has also earned a reputation for building fine long-distance trucks. Their trucks are coveted by many owner/operators, for whom owning a Kenworth is often the epitome of success. And that's no wonder, since over the years Kenworth has spent considerable time and money on improving driver comfort. During the early days of trucking they were the first to put thick padding under the trucker's bottom. Currently they are producing a kind of Hilton-on-wheels with the VIT—Very Important

Trucker—available as a conventional or the Aerodyne cab-over. VIT cabs are fitted with many conveniences one would expect in a costly hotel room.

The current fleet includes the W 900 conventional, introduced early in 1982, the K 100 cab-over, the C 500 Brute for construction jobs, the L 700 urban trucks, and the 900 line of heavy oilfield vehicles. They are built to the customer's specifications from a comprehensive list of drivetrain components.

The large Kenworth oil field trucks from the 900 series have "headache racks" behind the cab, containing a winch and spare wheel, and enormous V-radiators to ensure adequate cooling of the powerful engines, especially in desert areas.

Kenworth trucks made in Canada, Australia, and Mexico generally are the same models manufactured in the U.S. but with some local differences. In Canada, for example, the highway models are the same, but a special version of the C500 is manufactured there called the C550. It has two driven front axles in addition to the

rear tandem. Other Canada-only models are the LW 900 logger, the 850 mining truck, and the 849 and 840 oil field rigs. The Mexican Kenworth plant produces a special oil field truck developed for the Mexican state oil company, model W 924A. The Mexican plant also builds the L 700 for all Kenworth subsidiaries and sales in the U.S.

Significant models manufactured in Australia are the Transorient cab-over Kenworths and the SAR models, a conventional with a short, sloping hood.

L_ADER

A youngster among the great trucks is Leader, from Toowoomba, Australia, where production started early in 1972. In 10 years, Leader has established an impressive reputation and a bright future. They now have a nationwide sales network so Leaders can be bought and serviced in all parts of Australia.

A workforce of 50 people builds at least a truck per day. Among them is the original model, a ...laimer with front and rear tandem, four axles together. Meanwhile, the line has been completed with two- and three-axle trucks, either available with all-wheel drive or rear-wheel drive only. All are powered by Caterpillar diesel engines, though Detroit Diesel units may be specified as an option. Most axles, transmissions, and other major components are produced by local subsidiaries of major U.S. suppliers.

The Leader forward-control cab is the Australian fiberglass version of the American Mack cab. Fiberglass is the material preferred "down under." The latest novelty in the Leader range is the Challenger conventional, available complete with Western-style sleeper. It isn't designed for long hauls across Australia, with its limited power of only 200 HP from a Caterpillar diesel.

An interesting point about Leader trucks is that Allison automatic gearboxes were not offered as an option, but as standard equipment on the first models, though currently the Allisons are optional and Fullers are now the standard gearboxes.

Left: Leader 406 Overlander. *Right:* Leader Challenger 86-406 conventional.

LEYLAND

The company known today as Leyland is the result of many mergers, reorganizations, and the shutdowns of nearly a dozen famous makes of British commercial vehicles. It started during the '50s when Leyland bought Albion and Scammell, and made them subsidiaries of the Preston company. At about the same time another great company in British trucking, AEC, bought Maudslay, Crossley, and Thornycroft. Thornycroft's production was phased out, though trucks were built under that nameplate until the '60s, mainly with heavy models Mighty Antar, Big Ben, and Nubian.

Jaguar, still on its own, tried to broaden its scope by buying bus manufacturer Daimler and truck manufacturer Guy. In another British car group, BMC, the Austin and Morris truck lines were joined into one new BMC line. The Leyland Group took over AEC and its

Recent Leyland models: Constructor *(opposite page)*, Landtrain *(top)*, Roadtrain *(left)*, and Cruiser *(above)*.

subsidiaries. So Leyland, AEC, Scammell, Albion, Thornycroft, Maudslay, and Crossley became a unified force in the British and foreign truck markets. At about the same time, BMC and Jaguar joined forces to form British Motor Holdings, which included Guy, Austin and Morris. As a next move British Motor Holdings and Leyland Motor Corporation merged. Thus, British Leyland Motor Corporation was created. Now, after a dozen years of reorganizations and plant closings, two makes are left: Leyland and Scammell, the first one being a kind of melting pot of all those separate makes of the past, while Scammell operates independently as a custom builder.

Times have been tough for Leyland during recent years. The quality of their trucks waned during the '70s and the traditional export markets were largely lost to European, Japanese, and American competitors.

In Britain itself Continental truck manufacturers like Scania, Volvo, DAF, Mercedes, MAN, and Magirus successfully invaded the company's home market with trucks that were more modern and powerful than the antiquated Leyland designs. In a first attempt to turn the tide Leyland designed the Marathon during the '70s, a truck that no longer used only Leyland components. It could also be bought with Cummins diesel engines and Fuller transmissions and sold in some quantity in Great Britain, but did not sell well in Europe.

However, the Marathon was just an intermediate step to fill the gap between the old generation and a new generation of trucks being developed. The first model of the new generation was launched in 1980, the Roadtrain tractor, powered by a new Leyland Flexitorque diesel of 270 HP, coupled to a Spicer 10-speed gearbox of the splitter type. The cab was also new, designed by Ogle and

made for Leyland by Motor Panels, a company supplying cabs to nearly all British truck manufacturers and several abroad. With the Roadtrain, Leyland finally had a truck that was contemporary and in many respects ahead of the competition. It offered sound engineering and improved fuel economy, without losing speed or requiring special driving techniques.

The next of the new generation was the Cruiser, launched a few months later as a tractor for combinations up to 34 tons maximum, while the Roadtrain can cope with 40 tons. The third addition to the line is the Constructor, introduced in 1981 and available as a six- or an eight-wheeler and mainly intended for short-distance construction work. For the export business a new range of conventionals was developed called the Landtrain. These heavy models are for payloads up to 60 tons and are powered by Leyland or Cummins diesels.

LIAZ-SKODA

Oldest series in the Liaz-Skoda line is the 706 *(top)*. The S 100.55 *(left)* and the S 100.45 *(above)* are for long hauls.

Skoda has built trucks since 1907, though the company was called Laurin & Klement before 1925. When Czechoslovakian industry was nationalized after World War II, Liaz was founded and teamed with Skoda as the truck-building company. Of the three series of trucks currently made, the oldest is the 706, which dates back to the early '50s. It has been restyled and re-engineered since then, but it has retained its unusual feature of S-shaped frame rails instead of the more common

U-shape. Trucks and tractors in the 706 line are powered by a 242 HP Skoda diesel engine. Gross vehicle weight is 17 tons and the gross train weight is 33 tons. Like most Eastern European trucks, they feature roomy cabs built to accommodate crews of three or four persons.

The S100 line comprises Skoda's international haulers. Powered by a 310 or 344 HP Skoda diesel, they are available as a tractor or as a rigid truck and can haul gross train weights up to 38 tons. The newest

model is the 100.55, powered by a fuel efficient, turbocharged diesel rated at 305 HP. The interior features a driver's seat cushioned by a hydraulic shock absorber.

The 706 is also produced in Bulgaria under the Madara name and the 100.45 and 100.55 are sold in other European countries. Liaz-Skodas are regarded as hearty trucks designed to withstand the poor roads of Eastern Europe and climates that range from extreme cold to broiling heat.

MACK

"Built like a Mack truck" has been used as a sales slogan for 80 years and it apparently is still a good selling point. Mack currently ranks second in sales among Class 8 truck builders in the U.S., about four percentage points behind International, but ahead of companies such as GMC, Ford, and Freightliner. Mack tends to improve its share of the market when sales are slow, and sales of big trucks have indeed been slow in recent years. In 1979, 165,000 Class 8 trucks were sold in the U.S. It dropped to 102,000 in 1980 and less than 100,000 in 1981. Mack meanwhile, was increasing its share of the market to 18 percent in 1981. That wasn't enough to turn a profit, but Mack at least didn't have the heavy losses that International and White had to absorb that year.

Mack offers the right chassis for nearly every job. For highway work, they have the Cruise-Liner and the brand new Ultra-Liner, which replaced the popular F-series cab-over that was built from 1962 to 1981. Main powerplants in these trucks are the Mack Econodyne engines, usually coupled to Maxitorque transmissions. Cummins, Detroit Diesel, and Caterpillar engines can be ordered, as well as Fuller, Allison, and Spicer transmissions.

For on/off road service, Mack builds the DM series, workhorses of the construction industry. If more muscle is needed, the all-wheel drive DMM is available. The RM line was developed expressly for highway maintenance and also comes with all-wheel drive. The Super-Liner and RD series are designed for hauling heavy bulk loads either off-road or over the road. Best known of the Mack conventionals is the R-series, introduced in 1966, and a newer variant, the U-series, easily identified by its offset cab. The Value-Liner conventional is noted for being able to carry heavier loads than competitors because it is built with weight-saving materials. All these trucks are custom built, so buyers choose from a catalog filled with options. If you select all Mack parts, the familiar bulldog on the grille will be gold. Otherwise, it comes in chrome.

Mack trucks are built under license in Iran, Argentina, and Venezuela, and the company has its own plants in Canada and Australia. A French Mack was built in the former Bernard facilities, but this was a brief affair. Only a few were made and sold. The Canadian Mack line is about the same as the U.S. line, though some special models are offered, like the DMM 6006, a conventional with a driven tandem front and rear, and the RD 800. The Australian Mack fleet which started production in 1963, had greater variations. Up to 1980 they built a

Mack's newest cab-over, the plush and powerful Ultra-Liner. The Mack Econodyne diesel is standard.

Top: The Super-Liner, for heavy bulk loads. Other Macks (clockwise from above) include the DM, the R-series, Valu-Liner, and Australian MCR-600.

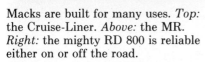

Macks are built for many uses. *Top:* the Cruise-Liner. *Above:* the MR. *Right:* the mighty RD 800 is reliable either on or off the road.

range of trucks differing in many respects from the American versions. Most significant was the forward control cab, which resembled the U.S. F-series cab, though it was made of fiberglass. Now, however, the Australian branch is a full subsidiary of Mack in the U.S., and the types produced are basically the same: the Cruise-Liner, the conventional R 600, and the MCR 600 low-forward.

For the future, Mack expects much

from a joint venture with Renault that has produced the Mid-Liner which quickly earned a reputation for outstanding fuel economy, day-to-day dependability, low maintenance, and easy servicing. A joint effort in the Class 8 field is in the works too, whereby Renault engineers will help Mack construct cabs and cab interiors unrivaled in the U.S., while Renault will get the excellent Mack Maxidyne engines in return for a new

generation of trucks to replace the R-range.

Mack trucks are used all over the world, with distributors for complete vehicles and parts in nearly every country. And in all these countries Macks are respected for the same reasons: they are sound trucks with excellent economy, and a positive influence on the bottom line of operating costs. Isn't that what trucking is all about?

MAN

Probably no truck manufacturer has more contracts and agreements with its competitors than MAN of West Germany. They once built light trucks jointly with SAVIEM, before that company joined forces with Berliet and became Renault Vehicules Industriels. Another agreement with Mercedes-Benz for manufacturing axles has lasted till now. The Hungarian Raba company manufactures MAN engines under license, in return delivering axles to the Munich plant. MAN has an agreement with the Romanian company Intreprinderea de Autocamioane Brasov to produce the Romanian trucks. The Yugoslav bus manufacturer Automontagge Ljubljana builds MAN buses under license, the Indian government produces MAN army trucks in its own plant under the Shaktiman name, the Turkish company Manas is partly owned by MAN, and MAN has assembly plants in South Africa, Pakistan, Indonesia, the Philippines, and Australia.

At home, MAN cooperates with VW to produce light and medium trucks, in Austria MAN owns the OAF and Graf & Stift companies, and in the U.S., MAN has a bus plant, founded after a joint venture with AM General was less fruitful than expected. And in Brazil, MAN-VW vehicles are produced in a former Chrysler plant acquired by Volkswagen. Again at home, MAN jointly owns the Motoren & Turbinen Union with Daimler-Benz.

Conclusion: MAN is one big truck manufacturer. In Germany, they rank second behind Mercedes in sales. They are the fifth largest manufacturer in Europe, offering a

wide range of conventional and cab-over trucks, ranging from 6.5 tons gross vehicle weight and up to about 250 tons gross train weight. They include platform-bodied trucks, tractors, tippers, dumpers, municipal chassis, chassis for special applications, chassis with underfloor engines, tandem-axled trucks, all-wheel-drive vehicles, four-axle trucks, and twin-steer trucks. The reason for MAN's success is no doubt their tradition of building advanced, reliable, high-quality vehicles, and their ability to construct fine diesel engines: muscular powerplants built with superb engineering.

Drivers like MAN trucks because of the roomy, comfortable cab and fine handling on the road. For long-distance truckers, sleeper cabs are available. MAN even has a special Middle East version with a small kitchen on the cab's engine cover.

MAN offers high performance at low engine stress and good fuel economy. That is one reason so many fleet owners quickly standardize on the make once they've bought one. Within the MAN conglomerate, OAF produces special vehicles, for example, a crash tender chassis, the heavy jumbo tractor with a 400 HP engine and 250 tons GTW, and the all-wheel-drive four-axle trucks with tandem axles front and rear. These giants are available with either a MAN or an OAF nameplate. The jumbos can have 4x2, 4x4, 6x2, 6x4, or 6x6 axle configuration and they are generally delivered as a semi-trailer tractor with additional ballast box that can be put over the fifth-wheel coupling, thus making the truck suitable for use as a prime mover.

MAN trucks are used all over Europe. An extra benefit the MAN trucker has on long runs is excellent service. Service agents are located all over the world and they can dispatch a complete workshop in a truck if that is necessary.

Opposite page: OAF 33.280 *(top)* and MAN 38.320 DFAK *(bottom). This page:* OAF Jumbo *(top right),* MAN 32.281 DHAK *(bottom right),* and MAN tractor with tank trailer *(below).*

MARMON

Top: Stunning Marmon conventional equipped with luxurious walk-in sleeper. *Left:* 86-P cab-over. *Above:* 54-P day cab.

Though Marmon is an old name in the American automobile industry, dating back to 1902, it was 61 years before the Marmon Motor Co. as we know it today came into being. In 1963 the truck manufacturing activities of Marmon Herrington Corporation were taken over by the Space Corporation, a subsidiary of the Interstate Insurance Corporation. Since then, they have handbuilt custom trucks particularly for the owner/operator.

Current Marmons were introduced in early 1982. Their most striking feature is the fancy exterior paint that is quite different from what usually comes from the factory. They also allow maximum flexibility for custom building on the technical side. They can be bought with any engine, any transmission, or any axle available, and in any wheelbase. Marmon's new conventionals and cab-overs feature all-aluminum, hand-crafted cabs, without any pressings. The conventional's hood is one-piece fiberglass. Interiors are fully padded, the floors covered with leaded vinyl floor mats.

All Marmons can, of course, be ordered in sleeper versions. In the cab-over, the sleeper is integrated into the cab. The conventionals have the well-known crawl-through sleeper box, or a walk-in sleeper with a height of 87 inches and comfort features like heater/air conditioner, TV set, digital clock, refrigerator, stereo system, and an inner spring mattress. For truckers who hate truck-stop food, a microwave oven is available to those who want to cook their own meals.

With all that hand crafting and luxury, a Marmon is one of the costliest trucks around, but one that can outclass even a Kenworth.

MERCEDES-BENZ

If anyone deserves the title of world's No. 1 truck manufacturer, it is Mercedes-Benz. They manufacture a wide range of trucks that without exception are at the top of their class, in all respects. Mercedes offers a limited range of engines, axles, transmissions, and cabs, but they can be blended into one of the most comprehensive truck lines in the world. The few types of trucks they don't make are made by others from components delivered by Mercedes. For example, heavy prime movers are built by the German specialist manufacturer Titan, using Mercedes-Benz components such as axles, engines, transmissions, and even cabs.

Key features of all Mercedes-Benz trucks are durability, reliability, excellent fuel economy, good driver accommodation, and the flexibility to tailor a vehicle to an operator's need, particularly at the upper end of the weight spectrum, where the requirements for customizing generally are the most demanding.

To maintain its position as the world's number one truck manufacturer, Daimler-Benz spends more than $400 million per year, or four percent of its revenue, on research and development. The current fleet of trucks was first introduced in 1973. Only a few models were available at that time, but M-B's highly efficient modular production system and the addition of new components allowed the line to be expanded almost annually, and Mercedes now offers more than 100 models of heavyweights alone. A big advantage of the modular production system is that it allows quick response to the changing demands of the market, or to changes in safety and construction regulations. Proven existing components can be rapidly redeployed into different configurations to meet new demands.

The heavy Mercedes cab-over trucks all use V-type engines: V-6, V-8, and V-10 units ranging in output from 190 to 380 HP. They combine performance and tractive power with very low fuel consumption. The heavy-duty truck range from Mercedes comprises rigids and tractors for local, medium-range and long-distance hauling. Gross combination weight in most countries is restricted to 38 tons by law, but technically these trucks are capable of hauling up to 100 tons. The lineup includes four-wheelers, six-wheelers with two driven rear axles or with one drive axle and one trailing axle, or steerable pusher axle, four-axle trucks with tandem sets at front and rear, the rear set being double driven or one driven axle in combination with a trailing axle. All-wheel-drive trucks are also available, though only in 4x4 and 6x6 configuration.

Besides the forward-control trucks Mercedes also manufactures a range of semi-conventionals with a short nose. They are intended for construction use, or as dumpers, mixer chassis, or quarry work. Many of these semi-conventionals are shipped disassembled to assembly plants all over the world, particularly those in the developing countries. Mercedes also has plants in Brazil and Argentina that were opened during the '50s. Both plants produce semi-conventional models. Those manufactured in Brazil are exported to the U.S., where CKD (completely knocked down) kits are assembled in Hampton, Virginia.

Over the years Mercedes has acquired several of its competitors. In Germany they bought the Krupp truck plant and the Hanomag-Henschel Company. Both were dismantled and the Hanomag-Henschel truck line consolidated with Mercedes. In the U.S. Mercedes owns the Euclid

The familiar Mercedes 3-point star is displayed on a variety of trucks. *Top:* a brawny model 2632. *Right:* Mercedes 3032. *Below, left:* the OM 422. *Below right:* a Mercedes LS 1418 on the road in the U.S.

construction machinery manufacturer, bought from White some five years ago, and the Freightliner Company, which was acquired in 1981. M-B recently bought the complete Swiss commercial vehicle industry. First FBW was acquired and reshuffled into a Mercedes subsidiary, where from 1983 on only four-axle Mercedes trucks will be manufactured and FBW production phased out. A few months later Saurer, the other Swiss truck maker, was bought, though it is uncertain what its fate will be. Mercedes has granted manufacturing licenses to FAP in Yugoslavia and to the Indian truck manufacturer Tata.

Mercedes trucks dominate the roads of Western Europe. Stand along a highway somewhere in Europe and you'll see one pass nearly every few minutes—massive construction trucks, impressive long-distance haulers, specialty trucks, all with the three-pointed star on the grille.

Right: Mercedes model 2419. *Right, center:* Mercedes Titan tractor. *Right, bottom:* A 2032 cab-over model with tank trailer. *Below:* Brazilian-built LS 1924.

59

MITSUBISHI

itsubishi, which means "Three Diamonds" in Japanese, has been in the vehicle manufacturing business for more than 65 years, though they didn't build their first commercial truck until 1932. Three years later they started Japan's first series of diesel-powered trucks under the Fuso name. Fuso was used for many years as the main name on most trucks, while Mitsubishi was displayed much more modestly. On recent models, however, Mitsubishi is the more dominant name and Fuso has been relegated to the side of the cab.

Mitsubishi builds well over 100 basic truck models, from light to heavy duty, and a line of crane carriers with lifting capacities up to 80 tons. For the entire range of trucks, three diesel engines are available; a 215 HP unit, a 280 HP unit, and a 310 HP powerplant.

Gearboxes are of the six speed or 10-speed splitter type. The interior of the cabs is spartan with bench seats and the driver's seat can only be adjusted fore and aft less than six inches.

Mitsubishi trucks are exported mainly to Third World countries, though for some time they also were available in Australia, sold by Chrysler as Dodge Fusos. But after Australian Chrysler operations were taken over by Mitsubishi imports of the heavy Fusos ended. Fusos are also produced under license in South Korea by the Dong A Motor Co., which offers a range of trucks and buses under its own name.

Left: Mitsubishi FU cab-over-engine.
Below: Heavy-duty Mitsubishi NR.

MOL

ot a drop of crude oil has ever been extracted from Belgian soil, yet the country is home for a leading specialist in the building of oil field trucks: Mol of Hoogledge. Gerald Mol started rebuilding military surplus trucks after World War II, fitting them with new bodies and sometimes adapting the chassis to a special purpose. When the supply of surplus trucks came to an end, Mol had a choice: concentrate completely on the other phase of his business, manufacturing truck bodies, or design his own trucks to replace the military vehicles. He eventually chose the latter, and in 1966 introduced a normal-control and a cab-over chassis, both using American axles and gearboxes, and a German air-cooled Deutz engine.

A whole line of special purpose vehicles has been developed since including all-wheel-drive off-highway trucks for hauling oil field equipment. The lighter models are still powered by Deutz air-cooled engines, but the big ones use Cummins diesels. These trucks are exported mainly to the Middle East, directly from Belgium or through the Mol subsidiary in Great Britain. Mol also makes heavy tractors for hauling loads up to 250 tons that are powered by Cummins diesels of 400 HP, or as an option, Detroit Diesel or Daimler-Benz engines. The heaviest vehicle in the current range is the TG 250 forward control 8x8 truck with tandem axle sets at front and rear. It is manufactured under license from the French company Perez & Raymond, the successors to the well-known French Willeme company that discontinued business some 15 years ago. Power for this vehicle comes from a 450 HP Cummins engine coupled to an eight-speed Clark Powershift transmission. With a load of 250 tons behind it, this truck can reach 12 mph. When unladen, the 28-ton TG 250 is capable of more than 35 mph. Mol also manufactures crane carriers and the famous Eagle buses, once produced in Belgium for export to the U.S., but now manufactured in Belgium for domestic use and for sales in Europe and the Middle East.

Above: Mol 5066. *Below:* Mol's heaviest, the TG 250. *Right:* Mol conventional.

NISSAN DIESEL

Nissan Diesel was founded in 1935 as the Nihon Diesel Industries Ltd., manufacturing 2-cycle diesel engines under a Krupp-Junkers license. Truck and bus production began after World War II with Nissan, the car makers, who bought a 40 percent share of the company. The Nissan Diesel name dates from 1960. In recent years they have scored major successes, for example, selling 2325 heavy duty logging trucks to the USSR in 1970 for use in Siberia, and a contract to produce marine diesels for Chrysler starting in 1968.

Nissan Diesel manufactures a wide range of trucks, both conventionals and cab-overs. They are stylish, powerful vehicles with a two-stroke diesel engine under the hood, ranging up to 45 tons gross train weight. Nissan Diesel trucks are used in Australia, New Zealand, South Africa, several European countries, and many Third World countries.

The recently introduced CW 45 and CW 52 ranges are modern trucks with well-designed, luxurious cabs and high technical standards. A number of them are already in service in Australia on the Stuart Highway, a majestic highway crossing the Australian continent, the home of the "roadtrains." The new Nissans have quickly built an excellent reputation. The CWA 45, a tandem-axle truck, is powered by a 275-HP diesel engine, also a two-stroker. Bolted to it is a six-speed gearbox or, as an option, a ten-speed splitter box. The CWA 45 is available as a truck or a tractor for a gross combination weight up to 45 tons. Fitted with a more powerful engine of more than 300 HP is the CW 52. Under the skin it is almost identical to the CW 45, and available in the same versions.

Heavy conventional models offered by Nissan Diesel are in the TW 52 series, not as sophisticated and driver-minded as the CWA 45 and CWA 52, but a tough workhorse that feels at home in the bush, the desert, swamps, or quarries. Specifically designed for hauling timber is the RZA r2 PP, which is in fact a TW 52, but with a longer wheelbase and fitted with a pole carrier and pole trailer. Nissan also manufactures crane carriers and a full line of light Nissan trucks that are sold by the parent company.

Left: Nissan Diesel CW 41
Right: Nissan Diesel CWA 45

OSHKOSH

From an area where much of the talk is about fishing, snowmobiling, and the Green Bay Packers comes a line of trucks that has few rivals in the world. Oshkosh builds heavy-duty giants that are intended to withstand snowstorms, deserts, extreme temperatures, and the roughest treatment. Oshkoshes have been renowned for these qualities since the company was founded in 1917. The company was originally launched by B. A. Mosling and William Besserdich, who earlier had been involved in FWD, another manufacturer of all-wheel-drive trucks.

Oshkosh manufactures a wide range of trucks, among them specialized vehicles like chassis for forward-discharge concrete mixers, fire engines, and complete airport crash tenders. But of greatest interest for most are the P, R, F, and J vehicles, true off-roaders that make their living on America's rural roads, in difficult winter conditions, on oil fields, hauling timber, and other arduous chores. Oshkoshes feature all-wheel drive, sturdy construction, and loads of power, so they have little trouble under such circumstances, and they continue to perform for 10 to 15 years, their

normal lifespan. F-series Oshkoshes are popular as construction trucks, carrying concrete mixers, dumper bodies, and brick platforms, since they're engineered for extreme service. Though the rear driving axles are acquired from the main axle manufacturers—Eaton and Rockwell—the front axle is built by Oshkosh. The front axle is often the weakest part of an all-wheel-drive truck; therefore, they designed their own so it could be built stronger.

The P-series of Oshkosh trucks are built specially for highway maintenance and snow removal. These sturdy 4x4 or 6x6 vehicles, powered by Caterpillar or Cummins engines up to 350 HP, also use an Oshkosh front driving axle, while the rear axles are Rockwell units. The real heavies are in the J-range, special desert transporters running on low-pressure tires, powered by engines up to 450 HP, and able to haul gross vehicle weights of some 70 tons. The most civilized vehicles in the Oshkosh line are the R-series on/off highway transporters, mainly used as tractors for hauling loads up to some 100 tons gross train weight. Oshkosh manufactures the K-series range of forward control 8x4 trucks with front and rear tandem axles for oil field use; GVW is 31 tons. Traction power is provided by a 400 or 450 HP diesel engine coupled to a five-speed automatic gearbox.

Oshkosh trucks can be found anywhere in the world, hauling

timber out of the Australian jungle, sugar cane in the Philippines, oil products in South Africa, drilling equipment in Saudi Arabia, and even complete factories. Four Oshkosh F-2365 tractors recently transported a complete desalination plant more than a mile from the coast to its place of operation in the desert of Saudi Arabia. The plant was delivered completely assembled by barge from Japan, on Scheuerle module trailers standing on 576 tires. Oshkosh trucks are also manufactured in South Africa. Once this was a very strong export market for Oshkosh and they built an assembly operation there. Later it became a manufacturing subsidiary, producing the R-series, and the E-series cab-over model that is still in production in the U.S. Now, however, the South African Oshkosh operation works under licenses granted by Oshkosh. The company is fully owned by the Barlow Rand group, a manufacturer of heavy construction machinery. The S-series conventional truck, a derivative of the R-series, is built in South Africa and fully assembled from components like Rockwell axles, Spicer clutches, Caterpillar engines, and Fuller transmissions. Also manufactured there is the E-series forward control range, in a 6x4 version, able to haul a gross combination weight of 68 tons. These vehicles frequently drive deep into inlands of Africa, often pulling two or three trailers.

Above left: Massive Oshkosh J "Desert King." *Above center:* F-series construction truck. *Above right:* Oshkosh F in use by a utility company. *Right:* R-series timber hauler. *Below right:* E 1244 C.O.E. built in South Africa. *Below left:* P-series in snow removal service.

PACIFIC

Three Canadians from the Vancouver, British Columbia, logging region decided in 1947 that there was a crying need for a custom-built truck that could efficiently haul timber from the woods down to the sawing mills. Consequently, Pacific Truck & Trailer was founded in a wharf shed in a Vancouver shipyard, starting production of a line of logging trucks and trailers for forest companies and owner/operators.

In 1970 Pacific was purchased by International Harvester, which built trucks up to some 60 tons gross combination weight, but didn't offer anything heavier or more specialized. The benefit for Pacific was that its line of trucks would be marketed worldwide through International Harvester sales outlets. Pacifics are now running in Australia, South Africa, New Zealand, and many more countries.

Four lines of trucks are currently offered, the P-500, the P-10, P-12, and P-16, all custom-built vehicles for heavy duty work in forests, oil fields, and as dumpers. A special version of the P-500 for highway operation has been developed called the Canadian. It is fitted with a fiberglass engine hood and a cab borrowed from the International Paystar.

An exclusive for New Zealand, an important market for Pacific, is the P-600 version of the Canadian, using a different engine hood and engineering adapted to New Zealand driving conditions. The Highway Locomotive was designed especially for heavy hauling. At least four are running in South Africa, owned by the road transport section of the South African Railways and used for hauling heavy loads that can't be split up. Each tractor has a GCW of some 200 tons, but they can be coupled to haul as much as 800 tons GCW.

Pacific P-12W

Pacific "Highway Locomotive"

PEGASO

Pegaso, or the Empresa Nacional de Autocamiones as the Spanish company is called officially, started truck production in 1946 in a plant owned by the Hispano-Suiza company. In 1955, a new line of five- and six-tonners went into production and it has expanded continuously with new models. Leyland acquired a majority interest in Pegaso in 1960, in return granting them license to produce Leyland diesel engines, at that time among the finest in the world, for the Pegaso trucks. A new line of trucks with the typical Pegaso sloping roof cab was introduced during the early '60s. For the first time Pegaso entered the multi-wheeler market with this line, offering a twin-steer six-wheeler and an eight-wheeler with single driven rear axle.

The current line of Pegaso trucks, with their angular cabs, was launched in 1972 and expanded since. In 1980 International Harvester acquired a 35 percent share of Pegaso and announced plans to extend it to a majority share within a few years.

Due to economic troubles at home, however, IH had to sell its Pegaso holdings to raise money.

Pegaso offers a broad range of vehicles—rigids, tippers and tractors, featuring 4x2, 6x2, 8x2, 6x4, and 8x4 drive. They are powered by six-cylinder diesel engines producing 200 to 352 HP. Pegasos are exported to South America, and to European countries such as Holland and Belgium. Pegaso trucks are solid, well-constructed, and stylish, with a comfortable cab. They are also attractively priced because wages are much lower in Spain than in the rest of Europe.

Pegaso 1180

Pegaso 1186

Above: M.A.N. C.O.E. with Anti-Lock Braking System (Germany) *Left:* M.A.N. Model 26.281 DF C.O.E. (Germany)

Far left: Marmon Model 60-P C.O.E. (U.S.A.) *Middle left:* Marmon Model 54-P Conventional with Walk-In Sleeper (U.S.A.) *Near left:* Mercedes-Benz 2628 C.O.E. (Germany) *Below:* A Mercedes-Benz convoy in the Sahara Desert

Above: Mitsubishi FUSO FV
C.O.E. (Japan) *Right:* Mol T
5264/05 Conventional (Belgium)
Upper right: Nissan Diesel UD
TWA 52 PH Conventional
(Japan) *Far right:* Nissan Diesel
UD CWA 45 C.O.E. (Japan)

This page: Top: Oshkosh P-Series 4-wheel-drive Conventional (U.S.A.) Above: Pacific Conventional (Canada) Right: Oshkosh S 1446 Conventional (South Africa) Page opposite: Above: Peterbilt Model 362 C.O.E. Tractor (U.S.A.) Below: Peterbilt Model 362 C.O.E. (U.S.A.)

Upper left: Peterbilt Model 359 Conventional (U.S.A.) *Lower left:* Peterbilt Model 387 Conventional (U.S.A.) *Above:* Peterbilt Model 359 Conventional (U.S.A.) *Below:* Pegaso Model 3180 C.O.E. (Spain)

Upper left: Raba U 16.256 C.O.E.
(Hungary) *Left:* Renault R 310 C.O.E.
(France) *Upper right:* Diamond Reo
Giant Model C 11664DB Conventional
(U.S.A.) *Above:* Saurer D 330
(Switzerland)

Page opposite: Top left: Scania do Brasil T 112 E Conventional (Brazil) Top right: Scammell Contractor Conventional (England) Middle left: Seddon-Atkinson C.O.E. (Australia) Middle right: Scania-Vabis R 112M and R 142H C.O.E. (Sweden) Bottom: Seddon-Atkinson 401 C.O.E. (England) This page: Above: Sisu SR 80 C.O.E. (Finland) Left: Spartan Motors/Emergency One C.O.E. Rescue Vehicle (U.S.A.) Below: Steyr Model 320 C.O.E. (Austria)

Page opposite: Top: Tatra 813 S1 (Czechoslovakia)
Lower left: Terberg F 1850 C.O.E. (Netherlands)
Lower right: Volvo F6-Series C.O.E. (Sweden)
This page: Top: Western Star High C.O.E.
(Canada) Above: Volvo N1023 Conventional
(Sweden) Right: Western Star Conventional
(Canada)

Right: White/Autocar
Construcktor Conventional
(U.S.A.) *Below:* White/
Autocar Conventional (U.S.A.)

PETERBILT

Peterbilt was established from the remnants of the Fageol Motors Co., once a famous West Coast truck and bus manufacturer. These remnants were acquired by Al Peterman, an energetic businessman who owned a lumber mill and a few vehicles that hauled timber to the mill. Peterman's business prospered in such a way that his fleet of trucks badly needed replacement and expansion. Since he was accustomed to doing everything himself, his first logging trucks were his own creations molded from commercial trucks. He thought he could produce the vehicles he needed from scratch, specialized logging trucks from the ground up. To achieve this, he bought Fageol and renamed it Peterbilt.

Over the years Peterbilt has earned recognition for building rugged haulers that can withstand the long inclines and tough climate of the West Coast states. Now part of the Paccar group, Peterbilt is the sister company of Kenworth. The two share some cabs and other components, but for the most part Peterbilt still makes its own trucks. Their most recent introduction is a completely new cab-over-engine 362 model launched early in 1981. Among the features of the newcomer are an aerodynamic shape that cuts wind resistance by nine percent compared to its predecessor, the 352. BBC dimensions available are 54, 63, 82, 90, and 110 inches. Interior features are a new gear shift system that eliminates the shift tower "island," a new air intake system from the cab's front, and a new air conditioning/heating system. An overhead console holds a stereo radio, antenna and wiring for CB, and the windshield defroster fans. Most distinctive exterior features are the single pane-flat windshield, the rectangular high-intensity headlights, and the marker lights and reflectors below the front skirt. Other models manufactured by Peterbilt are the 310, 348, 353, 359, 387, and 397. Of these, the 359 is the conventional companion of the 362 COE described above. Designed for real cross-country hauling, it is one of their most popular models, custom built to the last nut and bolt, and equipped with a plush interior that can be very tempting to the owner/operator.

The Model 353 is the Peterbilt for bone-breaking off-road work like mining, construction, logging, heavy equipment hauling, and oil field transport. Peterbilt's largest conventional is the 387, a muscular brute that can tackle any job and take the punishment of extremely heavy loads. Any engine, transmission, or axle can be mounted in the heavy-duty chassis frame. Model 348 is a special vehicle for mixer operation and other construction jobs. Its sloping nose makes it easy to maneuver and it's fitted with a comfortable cab.

The 310 is Peterbilt's smallest model, though it still offers an impressive payload. It is designed for

Peterbilt's new C.O.E., the sleek 362

The Peterbilt 352 C.O.E. *(top and bottom photos)* was a popular long-distance model for many years. It has been replaced by the more aerodynamic 362. *Center photo:* The lighter-weight 310 C.O.E.

Above: The 359 is Peterbilt's newest cross-country conventional, a custom built beauty and companion to the 362 C.O.E. *Left:* the 353 is designed for back-breaking duty like mining and construction.

urban work like sanitation, street washing, municipal maintenance jobs, or for pick up and delivery duties. Like most U.S. manufacturers Peterbilt offers buyers a wide range of optional engines, transmissions, and axles so they can write their own specifications.

A few years ago Peterbilt tried, like Kenworth, to get a foothold in Australia, a country well suited to the American heavyweights. The Australian "truckies" (as they are called down under), however, were Kenworth-minded from the moment that marque was made available in their country. They did not have the same appreciation for the Peterbilt and very few were sold. Eventually, Paccar decided to concentrate completely on Kenworth in Australia. Peterbilt conventionals for construction work are exported on a small scale to South American countries and the Philippines for the logging industry and hauling sugar cane. And that is exactly the kind of work Al Peterman had in mind for his trucks when he designed the first one.

RABA

The Hungarian company Raba has manufactured commercial vehicles and parts since 1910, though, strangely enough, they never designed a vehicle themselves. Instead, they have always produced foreign trucks under license. At first they were Praga five-tonners, then Krupps, and by 1928 the Austro-Fiat truck, and in 1937 MAN diesel engines for trucks, and a diesel-engine MAN bus.

In 1963, another license agreement with MAN was reached, allowing Raba to produce modern MAN diesel engines and driven rear axles, in addition to their own line of axles. Building engines and axles gave Raba a good start towards production of complete vehicles. This step was taken in 1970, when the contract with MAN was broadened to include the licensed production of trucks.

Raba manufactures two- and three-axle vehicles in various sizes, but in only a few basic models. For example, the Raba 831 has a gross vehicle weight of 16 tons, gross combination weight of 38 tons, and a payload of about 9 tons in the 4x2 version. It can also be had with a tag axle, however. In the 6x2 configuration the payload of the truck is 13 tons. Power is supplied by a 230 HP inline six MAN-Raba diesel engine. The transmission is by ZF or Fuller. Raba's 6x2 and 6x4 heavy tractors are the LI 16.256, the 833, and the 853. Powered by engines of 230 and 256 HP, they are used for international hauling duty.

In 1981 Raba reached an agreement with DAF of Holland, by which DAF would buy axles from Raba and in return Raba would use DAF cabs on its trucks. At the same time the model lineup was reshuffled and enlarged. It now includes the F 16 4x4 truck with 256 HP Raba-MAN diesel, the F 22 and S 22 ranges, rigids and tractors in 6x2 configuration, with a payload of 13 tons GCW. The S 16 4x2 tractor payload is 38 tons GCW and the F 26 and S 26 6x4 rigids and tractors are rated for 42 tons GCW. The engine for all these models is the Raba-MAN 256 HP powerplant.

Raba S 22 6 x 2

Raba 833.13, long-distance C.O.E. from Hungary

RENAULT

For the first time in 25 years, the Renault name appeared on heavy trucks in 1980. Since the company was formed in 1899 commercial vehicles had been a mainstay, but in 1955 the Renault truck manufacturing activities were merged with those of Latil and Somua, and with the bus manufacturing activities of Chausson, Floirat, and Isobloc to form SAVIEM. Societe Anonyme de Vehicules Industriels et de Mecanique is the new company's full name, but it probably has never slipped over anybody's tongue. This giant combine never really flourished, however, and in 1974, Renault acquired Berliet, an ailing French truck manufacturer, and a few years later established Renault Vehicules Industriels. Integration of the two model lines and production took several years and was completed in 1980. From that date on the Berliet and SAVIEM names were dropped and Renault was revived as a truck name. An aggressive export policy was also started. Renault affiliates were established in Great Britain, Belgium, Austria, and Germany, and distributors were established in many other countries. In 1981 Renault acquired a 50 percent share of the truck manufacturing operations of Peugeot and the British and Spanish Dodge lines. Earlier Renault had bought 20 percent of the Mack truck stock and agreed to produce the Mid-Liner, a medium-duty truck derived from the Renault J-series, for the American company.

Renault now manufactures four series, the J-series of light and medium cab-overs, the G-series of medium and heavy cab-overs, the R-series of highway cab-overs, and

Opposite page: Renault R 350
highway C.O.E. with special paint.
This page: R 306 *(top)*, GBH 280
dump truck *(left)*, TR 306 *(below
left)*, and the TF 231 *(below right)*.
The TR and TF models have
turbocharged diesel engines.

the GBH series of conventionals for
construction duty. The J and G series
were inherited from SAVIEM, while
the other two come from Berliet.
Gross combination weight is up to 38
tons in the G range and engine
output is 216 HP. The R series has
the real heavies, powered by 306 or
356 HP diesel engines and, in the
tractor version, GCWs up to some
180 tons. The cab of the R-series is
an appealing, impressive creation.
The shell is also used by Ford on the
Transcontinental. Within the Renault
cab the long-distance trucker finds
plenty of comfort, a clean,
well-designed dashboard, a large
sleeping area in the night versions,
and a comfortable seat.

The GBH model is the truck for
the extra tough job. It's a real
off-roader in 6x4 or 6x6 versions, a
strong base for a concrete mixer,
dumper, or off-road tractor, and for
export to developing countries, where
such a robust truck is highly
welcome. Renault manufactures
about 100,000 commercial vehicles
per year, 50,000 in completely
knocked down form for export.

SAURER

Saurer made its first car in 1896 and then turned its attention to manufacturing trucks, starting in 1903 with a five-tonner. This and following designs were so successful that Switzerland-based Saurer started manufacturing subsidiaries in Austria and France, while in Germany MAN started truck production under a Saurer license. For some time Saurer also had a plant in New Jersey and a Saurer truck was one of the first to cross the U.S. continent. The U.S. plant eventually was acquired by Mack. Saurer was among the first to conduct research on diesel engines and produce them for use in trucks and buses.

Saurer was recently acquired by Daimler-Benz. What the consequences will be is yet unclear. Currently, Saurer manufactures vehicles only under its own nameplate, a wide range of 4x2, 4x4, 6x2, 6x4, 6x6, and 8x4 models. They are powered by diesel engines from 250 to 315 HP and use a limited range of axles and other components that can be matched in many configurations to produce a broad range of vehicles.

Cab-over-engine and conventional versions are available, the latter using a fiberglass hood. Conventional Saurers are mainly used for construction work and heavy hauling. They can handle about 100 tons in a 6x6 version.

Saurers are extremely well-built vehicles. Lifespans of 20 or more years are common and many older Saurers are still performing their duties in Switzerland. So even if the production of Saurer trucks is soon discontinued, the last Saurer probably won't disappear from Swiss roads before the year 2010.

Saurer D 330 BF 4x4

Saurer D 330 BF 8x4

SCAMMELL

For more than half a century Scammell has maintained a reputation for being one of the best trucks makers in Britain. They initiated some classic truck designs, like the rigid and the articulated eight-wheeler. In 1929 they introduced the world's first 100-tonner, an articulated truck. Famous British hauling contractors such as Pickfords used these trucks, which were powered by a surprisingly small 60 HP gas engine. Scammell Lorries was incorporated in 1922, and became part of Leyland in 1955.

At the start of the '60s Scammell introduced the classic Routeman, which was built with a ribbed plastic cab until quite recently. The Contractor tractor was launched in 1965 and produced in substantial numbers for home and overseas clients. The current generation of forward-control Scammells started in 1968 with the introduction of the 6x4 Crusader, later also available in a 4x2 version, both only as a tractor.

The LD 55 bush tractor, a spartan vehicle for export to the Third World, and the Nubian line of all-wheel-drive chassis for fire and crash tenders, were taken over from Thornycroft production and added to Scammell's. Recent production changes include the T 45 Constructor models, 6x4 and 8x4 trucks for the construction business, and successors to the Scammell Routeman and certain Leyland models. The Scammell nameplate does not appear on these new models; they are sold only as Leylands.

Though Scammell can produce vehicles for special order, they are not really custom builders. The differences in specifications and equipment on various models are limited. They mount diesel engines from Leyland, Rolls-Royce, and Cummins, along with Fuller and Allison gearboxes. The latest model with the Scammell nameplate is the S 24, a heavy duty 6x4 truck and tractor chassis for combined on/off road work. One of the interesting options available on this vehicle is a torque converter mated with a manual transmission. The biggest current Scammell is the Commander tank transporter powered by a 625 HP Rolls-Royce V-12 diesel engine, an optimum combination of power and strength.

625-HP Commander, Scammell's biggest

Scammell Routeman, a British classic

SCANIA

Two of the biggest, most powerful cab-overs offered by Scania are the R 142 M *(right)* and the R 142 E *(below)*. The T 112 H *(below right)* is built for heavy-duty work like construction.

Scania is one of the oldest truck manufacturers in the world and has built trucks continuously since 1897. Starting in 1927, Scania concentrated on heavy models, though the heaviest truck in those days had a capacity of only five or six tons. Diesel-powered commercial vehicles have been their main product since 1931. Today, Scania manufactures about 27,000 vehicles a year, most of them truck chassis, and most components used are their own. Complete vehicles are produced at plants in Sweden, Holland, Brazil, and Argentina.

The nucleus of the production are three basic types of diesel engines with displacements of 8, 11, and 14 liters. They are available in turbocharged or normally aspirated versions, while the smallest engine can also be ordered with an intercooler. The smallest engines are installed in conventional and cab-over versions of the series 82.

The medium engines are under the hoods of the 112 range and the largest engines are mounted in the 142 series vehicles. Most vehicles in these ranges are available in 4x2, 6x2, 6x4, 8x2, or 8x4 axle configuration.

Scania's chassis are divided into three main strength classes: M (medium duty), H (heavy duty), and E (extra heavy duty). These classes harmonize with carrying and strength requirements for various transport operations. This way, a buyer can select a lighter chassis for a long-distance vehicle that will travel over good roads. For more strenuous hauling, like forestry work, the H and E chassis can be specified. Conventional trucks (identified with the suffix T) have a forward tilt hood of reinforced plastic and are available in day or night versions. Gearboxes available are a 5- and a 10-speed unit. A wide range of rear axle ratios are offered to meet torque and speed requirements. The cab-overs are

designated G, P, and R, the G having a low build while the P offers the greatest ground clearance. The R is the largest cab in the range, a night version able to take the 14-liter engine.

The Scania 112 chassis is designed for intensive use on either short or long distances.

The series 142 is one of the most robust and powerful Scania models and is available in cab-over and conventional versions. The powerplant is the 14-liter V-8 engine, producing 388 HP at 2000 revs. This truck is frequently used for hauling extremely heavy loads, so the 10-speed gearbox has an extremely low bottom gear of 13.51:1 to enable starting under awkward conditions.

A typical Scandinavian feature on Scanias is a lift device for the trailing axle, that allows it to be lifted on icy or rough roads to provice greater traction, reduced tire scrub, and tighter turning radius.

Scania T 112 H

Scania G 112 M

SEDDON-ATKINSON

At the beginning of the '70s Seddon and Atkinson were two flourishing but rather traditional British manufacturers of trucks. Seddon built "lighter" heavy trucks while Atkinson concentrated on the real heavies. In 1970 a takeover battle was fought over Atkinson between ERF, Foden, and Seddon, and the battle was finally won by Seddon. A new company, Seddon-Atkinson, was established, but each make still built its old lines of trucks. It wasn't until 1975 that a new joint line of trucks started with the introduction of the 400, which had a new cab that was a giant leap forward in U.K. standards of truck comfort. British truckers until then were accustomed to spartan cabs that lacked comfort, but with the arrival of the Seddon-Atkinson 400, this changed instantly, and sales of the new model went sky-high.

The year before, International Harvester had become the new owners of the company and, Seddon-Atkinson developed into a major force on the British truck market. Its annual output of some 5000 trucks is more than the combined production of ERF and Foden and more than either Bedford's or Ford's production of heavy trucks.

The 400 models have since been replaced by the 401, introduced in 1980. The most striking appearance feature of the new vehicle is the big Atkinson "A" revived from the past and mounted in the middle of the grille. The name Atkinson and the "A" badge had such legendary impact on old truckers that it was a wise marketing decision to emphasize these again. The 401 is available only as a tractor, powered by Gardner, Cummins, or Rolls-Royce engines of 214 to 320 HP, coupled to a Fuller Roadranger gearbox. The rear axle is a Seddon Atkinson unit. For heavy rigid operations the 400 is still available, with 4x2, 6x4, and 8x4 chassis, powered by Gardner, Cummins or Rolls-Royce diesels of 193 to 256 HP. Gross combination weight of the 401 is 40 tons, while the 400 can handle 32 tons. Where less power is needed, Seddon-Atkinson offers the 300, a line that consists of a tractor and three rigids: 4x2, 6x4, and 8x4. Power comes from an International diesel engine that produces 196 or 214 HP.

International Harvester of Australia manufactures the Atkinson F 4870, continuing the success Atkinson had "down under" with its American-style custom-built cab-overs.

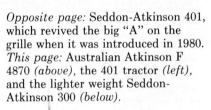

Opposite page: Seddon-Atkinson 401, which revived the big "A" on the grille when it was introduced in 1980. *This page:* Australian Atkinson F 4870 *(above)*, the 401 tractor *(left)*, and the lighter weight Seddon-Atkinson 300 *(below)*.

SISU

Sisu is the Finnish word for guts, nerve, and stubbornness, and it must be said that the founders of this company have showed a lot of it. In 1931, the Suomen Autoteollissuus was founded against the advice of experts who were unanimous in their opinions: a truck maker couldn't survive in Finland because the market was too limited and the available capital was too scarce. But the company survived those early years, and in 1942 a subsidiary was founded, the Yhteissisu Oy, which later would become Vanaja, the second Finnish truck manufacturer, which existed until 1968, when the two firms merged.

Sisu's ownership is divided three ways: 84 percent is state owned, 10.5 percent of the stock is owned by Saab-Scania, and 5.5 percent is owned by British Leyland. They use Finnish Valmet diesel engines as the standard powerplant for their trucks, but Cummins or Rolls-Royce diesels can be installed as options. The whole line of Sisu vehicles is very specialized, filling in the gaps left by the larger manufacturers and adapting their vehicles to special needs and circumstances.

A complete revision of the company's offerings was initiated in 1980 with the design of new cab-over and conventional cabs that were gradually fitted on all models, which at the same time were being overhauled technically. Still in production from the old generation are the multi-axle models like the Sisu M 6x2 and 8x2 cab-overs, powered by Cummins diesels of 375

to 405 HP output. They are frequently used in the logging industry, hauling pinewood from the far north of Finland to the mills on the coast. Normal control models are used for the same jobs, and also for construction and quarry work, such as the R-range 6x2 trucks, powered by Cummins or Rolls Royce diesels from 325 to 375 HP.

The SR models are their new conventionals, available with Cummins diesels of 290 to 400 HP. The new SK cab-over models are powered by a 214 HP Valmet diesel engine. The SC 150 is fitted with a forward set, low-mounted cab and is intended for sanitation work. It has a 197 HP Valmet diesel coupled to an Allison automatic gearbox. Sisu trucks have smart-looking cabs, and if that is the reason someone selects a truck, it should be an easy job for the Sisu people to sell one of theirs.

Sisu M 8x2, rugged Finish C.O.E.

Sisu SK, new 214-HP C.O.E.

SPARTAN

Spartan Motors of Charlotte, Michigan, was incorporated in 1975 and began turning out heavy trucks the following year. But that doesn't mean the people of Spartan Motors are new to the truck-building industry. Nearly all of the firm's workers are veterans of Diamond Reo, a truck company that was owned for many years by White Motor Corporation. Reo was started in 1908 by Ransom E. Olds, who is best known for developing the Oldsmobile car. When Diamond Reo was sold by White a few years ago, a number of Diamond Reo management and production employees founded Spartan, creating

a new marque in the highly competitive arena of heavy-truck manufacturing. (Diamond Reo trucks are now built by Osterlund, Inc., of Harrisburg, Pennsylvania.)

Because it is a new make, Spartan is one of the smallest truck manufacturers, concentrating on specialized vehicles such as fire engines, off-road haulers, and custom-made over-the-road trucks. Spartan also builds specialized derrick trucks used by utility companies to bore post holes.

Early models were the two-axle 2000 chassis that could be used for fire engines or trucks and the HH-1000 6x4 coal hauler with a load capacity of 40 tons. The newer 3000 series has tandem rear axles. Base engine in the cab-over 2000 and 3000 is a Detroit Diesel with a gross horsepower rating of 239. The

transmission is a Spicer 5-speed and the axles are Rockwell. Engines with power up to 492 horsepower are available, as are 6-speed automatic and 7-speed manual transmissions. Maximum gross vehicle rating on the 3000 series is 35 tons. Also optional is a deluxe "Red Baron" interior that has a swing-out instrument panel for easier service.

Spartan CFC 2000 fire truck chassis

STEYR

Steyr, which has produced trucks in Austria since 1922, merged with Saurer's truck operations in Austria during the early '60s. From this marriage a completely new range of trucks evolved—attractive, powerful, heavy vehicles from 4x2 to 8x4 axle configuration for all kinds of jobs. This series was updated and technically improved a few years ago and is now known as the Steyr 91 series. About 25 models are offered within this series. Power is by diesel engines producing from 145 to 320 HP. They're not really quick runners, but speed isn't needed in the mountains of Austria.

The tilt-cab mounted on these vehicles has an advanced wedge shape, introduced in 1968, though in those days was much more striking in appearance than it is now. Steyrs are exported all over Europe and to many more distant countries. Steyr has license agreements with a number of Eastern European manufacturers who build Steyr engines and other parts.

Weight and length regulations are tougher in Europe than in the U.S., so a new kind of night cab has emerged, and Steyr was one of the first to offer it as a regular feature on its vehicles. The sleeper has been placed on top of the cab, where it functions as a bed for the driver and also as an air-deflector for improved aerodynamics. Such top sleepers are generally made out of fiberglass, which is lighter than steel.

Among European truck manufacturers, Steyr is a small but inventive company, with a fine range of vehicles that keeps the company's sales at a profitable level. Though they have contracts with Daimler-Benz, it has not yet been necessary for them to seek financial protection from this big brother.

Steyr 1390 cab-over-engine

Steyr 1890 cab-over engine

TATRA

Nesselsdorfer, the forerunner of Tatra, started producing vehicles in the village of Nesselsdorf in 1897, when it was part of Austria. After World War I the village became part of Czechoslovakia and was renamed Koprivnice. At the same time the name of the Nesselsdorfer vehicles was changed to Tatra, after the neighboring mountain range. A unique Tatra car was developed in 1919 by Hans Ledwinka using a backbone chassis instead of the usual ladder frame. A truck version of this vehicle was introduced four years later and this type of chassis is still used on all Tatra vehicles, no matter if they have two, three or four axles. Tatra produces about 8000 commercial vehicles a year. Other features of Tatra trucks are the use of air-cooled diesels, and permanent all-wheel drive.

Two series of vehicles are currently offered, the conventional 2.148 series and the 813 cab-overs. The 148 started production during the early '60s but since then has undergone a number of changes to modernize it. Power is supplied by a V-8 diesel engine of 212 HP, in conjunction with a five-speed gearbox and a two-speed auxiliary transmission. The suspension is independent all around. Each wheel is mounted on a half axle that is hinged on the backbone chassis. The 148 is available as a tipper, with platform body, or as an articulated tractor; gross combination weight is 37 tons.

The 813 cab-over was launched in 1967 in four versions, a 4x4 truck, a 6x6 truck with tandem axle at rear, a 6x6 truck with front tandem, and an 8x8 truck. In general, the construction is the same as the 2.148. The only difference is the engine, which in the 813 is a V-12 unit giving 270 HP. The 813 6x6 is capable of pulling trailers up to 100 tons, with excellent driving properties even under the most difficult conditions, like ice-packed roads.

Currently under development is a completely new range of cab-over diesels to eventually replace the 2.148, which after nearly 25 years of service is due for retirement.

Tatra 2.148 features independent suspension.

Tatra 813 S1 cab-over-engine

TERBERG

Terberg, the Dutch truck manufacturer, started as a village forge in 1870 and built carriages during the early 20th century. They didn't enter the truck field until 1945, when they started rebuilding surplus army trucks for local clients, adapting military vehicles to civilian uses. This rebuilding business evolved into remanufacturing during the early '60s. Surplus army trucks were completely disassembled, all parts overhauled, and installed on new trucks fitted with Mercedes or DAF diesel engines and a new, coach-built cab.

Gradually, all the military components were replaced by new components, like Rockwell axles, DAF engines, Raba axles, and ZF transmissions. Thus, Terberg grew into a real truck manufacturing business, a custom builder in the true sense of the word, since every truck could be completely tailored to the customer's needs. For some years Terberg mounted Mercedes semi-conventional cabs on its trucks, powering them with Mercedes diesels. Currently, however, Terberg uses Volvo cabs and engines, both forward control and normal control. As a result of a marketing deal, Volvo distributes Terberg vehicles in a number of other countries. Terberg produces the F 1550 6x2 trucks with steered tag axle, the F 1850 8x4 truck or tractor, the F 1150, SF 1350, F 1900, and F 2000 4x4, 6x6 and 8x8 vehicles, all powered by Volvo engines of 200 to 330 HP. The clutch and gearbox generally also are of Volvo construction, but the axles are made by Terberg.

Annual production is between 500 and 550 units, of which about 70 percent are exported as far away as Argentina, one of the 70 countries where Terbergs are used.

Terberg SF 1350 250 HP conventional

Terberg F 2000 C.O.E.

VOLVO

Volvo is an industrial titan, building a variety of products in its many Swedish plants that includes cars, buses, and a wide range of trucks, from city delivery vehicles to international haulers. They have built trucks since 1928 and Volvo has initiated several innovations in Europe, like the first turbocharged diesels in the early '50s, and American-style cab-overs in 1962. Volvo is the fifth largest manufacturer of heavy-duty diesel trucks in the world, producing well over 20,000 trucks each year, all fitted with their own engines, transmissions, and axles.

The current line of trucks has been phased in since 1977, the year the F10 and F12 replaced the F86/F88. Particular attention has been paid to long-distance driver comfort, since most Volvo heavies are used on longer routes. Air conditioning is standard equipment, the steering wheel is adjustable, and the

Opposite page: A pair of F12 Volvos powered by 350 HP turobodiesels being tested in Sweden. *This page:* The F7 Turbo C.O.E. *(above),* semi-conventional N1023 6x4 tractor *(above right),* and a luxurious F12 Globetrotter *(right).*

passenger side window is an electrically operated power unit. The F10 is available in 4x2 or 6x2 versions, both powered by either a 300 HP turbocharged diesel engine or a 250 HP normally aspirated engine. Maximum train weight of the tractor is 52 tons.

The big brother F12 is available as a 4x2 tractor or rigid (70 and 52 tons gross combination weight, respectively), a 6x2 rigid, also 70 tons GCW, and a 6x4 truck or tractor with 100 tons GCW. Power is supplied by a 350 HP turbocharged diesel. The N-series covers 4x2, 6x2, and 6x4 models with a semi-conventional cab and three diesel engines up to 300 HP.

The intermediate heavies are in the F7 series, introduced in 1978, and the lightweights are in the F6 series. Volvo describes the F7 as a blend of reliability and comfort, with the

power of the former F86 coupled to the driving ease and safety of the newer F10/F12. Features like a built-in air conditioner are also found on the F7, as well as other comfort items. Two engines are available, a turbocharged 202 HP engine, and a 217 HP version with turbocharger and an intercooler. The semi-conventional N7, N10 and N12 are the workhorses among the Volvos, intended for short distance work, on- or off-road. Designed solely for use in Switzerland, a country with its own trucking regulations, is the Volvo CH 230, with a maximum cab width of 230 cm (90 inches). The CH 230 is available as a 4x2, 6x2, 6x4, or 8x4 chassis, powered by a 308 HP turbocharged diesel engine coupled to an 8-speed gearbox. The gross train weight is 65 tons.

The main Volvo manufacturing facilities are of course in Sweden.

The company also has plants in Belgium and Brazil, and an assembly operation in Australia, where Volvos are adapted to local needs and laws. Another assembly operation is maintained in Great Britain for the CH 230 and other Volvos, and an 8x4 is made for sale in Great Britain and Switzerland.

Volvo is also trying its luck on the American market. After a lengthy agreement with Freightliner had to end because Freightliner was bought by Daimler-Benz, Volvo acquired the bankrupt White Motor Co. The White group was completely reorganized; new plants were occupied and parts of the group were disposed of, like Western Star, which is now on its own. White trucks are assembled in a plant in Virginia and from September 1982 on, Volvo F7 models have also been produced in this plant.

Left: a sampling of the variety offered by Volvo. *Below:* The F6 Turbo, lightest of Volvo's heavyweights.

WESTERN STAR

When White Trucks went bankrupt several months ago, the Canadian Western Star plant became independent. Production of Western Star cab-overs and conventionals will continue as before and they will still be available through White dealers, since White and Western Star agreed to this arrangement. Western Star was founded as a separate marque within the White group during the late '60s, in response to a need for powerful, custom-built trucks in a distinctive Western style. White wasn't the only one to establish a special "Western" make. Mack did so too, to meet the needs of the construction industry and loggers.

Western Stars are hand-made trucks, bolted together with the intention they should tackle the toughest jobs either on or off the road. The cab-over has an aerodynamically designed cab with rounded corners to reduce fuel use. Its interior offers plenty of space and sumptuous luxury. All electrical connections are centralized in the TEC (Truck Electrical Center). The same control module contains all the air connections, simplifying service and repair.

The conventional Western Star is a real trucker's truck. It can be customized to taste and to special driving needs. It is available as a heavy duty truck or tractor, in a 4x2, 6x4, or all-wheel-drive configuration, and with a wide choice of engines, transmissions, and axles.

Big, bold, and built to last, the custom-made Western Star conventional is roomy and luxurious with a distinctive Western style and up-to-date technology.

WHITE

Serious economic problems forced White Trucks into bankruptcy in the late '70s and the chances for recovery looked grim. For the Swedish Volvo group, buying

White was an excellent chance to retain and even improve their position in the U.S. truck market, a position they had created through cooperation with Freightliner. The deal was settled in early 1981 and in September a new truck manufacturer, Volvo White Truck Manufacturing Company, was announced.

The new company did not take over the whole White group integrally. Volvo was interested in White and Autocar, but since Western Star was less attractive, its Canadian operations were sold to a group of private investors. White would market Western Star trucks in the U.S., but was no longer interested in producing them. Whites are being

Above: White Road Boss 2. *Below:* Custom conventional from Autocar division. *Below right:* White Road Xpeditor.

Clockwise, from top left: Australian Road Boss, U.S.-built Road Boss 2, Road Boss, and Road Commander C.O.E.

manufactured in a plant in Dublin, Virginia, while Autocars are being built in Ogden, Utah. All trucks are built to the customer's requirements from the usual list of engines.

A new feature on the conventional Road Boss is the White Integral Sleeper, offering an aerodynamic design on the outside and spacious, luxurious sleeping quarters inside. The cab is mounted on a rear airbag to enhance comfort.

Over the years, White became a dominant factor in the transportation field with well-made trucks that earned a reputation for dependability and ingenuity. White once was strong in the "Western" market because Freightliner allowed White to sell Freightliners under the White

Freightliner name. When Freightliner left the fold, a gap was created in the White product line. White wanted to fill it with a new model to be built at a huge new plant that would be erected especially for this truck, but it never got that far. White concentrated instead on its existing models, the Road Boss 2 conventional, the Road Commander 2 cab-over, the Road Xpeditor city truck, the Autocar models, and Western Star series. Slumping sales, however, meant trouble for the company, as did the lack of a light truck. Talks with Volkswagen and MAN from Europe were conducted to foster cooperation in this field, but no agreements were reached. MAN at one time held 12.6 percent of the

White stock and was planning to increase it to 51 percent, but these plans were later cancelled.

White also operates a manufacturing plant in Australia, producing the Road Boss and Road Commander models in a version adapted to Australian needs. The usual range of engines, transmissions, and axles is available to design a truck of individual specifications, a move that has proved popular with many Australian "truckies." About 400 trucks are produced annually. However, when the American White operation went bankrupt, the Australian daughter also went into receivership, and it is uncertain whether White Australia will continue to exist.